P9-CQE-075

THE DECLINE AND CRASH
OF THE AMERICAN ECONOMY

Futurecasting

RCDC: Regional Cooperation Among Developing Countries (with Ervin Laszlo and A. K. Bhattacharya)

The Soviet Union, Eastern Europe, and the New International Economic Order (edited with Ervin Laszlo)

The Structure of the World Economy (edited with Ervin Laszlo)

Food for the World (with Toivo Miljan and Ervin Laszlo)

World Leadership and the New International Economic Order (with John O'Manique and Ervin Laszlo)

The United States, Canada, and the New International Economic Order (with Ervin Laszlo)

Political and Institutional Issues and the New International Economic Order (with Ervin Laszlo)

No More Dying

Sweet Bobby

Crown of Flowers

JOEL KURTZMAN

THE DECLINE AND CRASH OF THE AMERICAN ECONOMY

W. W. Norton & Company / New York London

LIBRARY OF CONGRESS CATALOGING-IN-PUBLICATION DATA

Kurtzman, Joel.
  The decline and crash of the American economy / by Joel Kurtzman.
    p.   cm.
  Includes index.
  1. United States—Economic conditions—1981– 2. United States—
Economic policy—1981– 3. Budget deficits—United States.
4. United States—Dependency on foreign countries. I. Title.
HC106.8.K87 1988
338.973—dc19   87-33772

ISBN 0-393-02523-3

W. W. Norton & Company, Inc., 500 Fifth Avenue, New York, N.Y. 10110
W. W. Norton & Company Ltd., 37 Great Russell Street, London WC1B 3NU
1 2 3 4 5 6 7 8 9 0

This book is dedicated
to Susan and Eli with love
and with high hopes
for the future.

CONTENTS

INTRODUCTION

IN THE current American economy, wishful thinking has replaced analysis. While we live in the delusional kingdom of
Reaganomics, Japanese and European companies are grab-
bing larger shares of what were once our primary markets
both at home and abroad. In the past seven years our trade
balance has deteriorated from a $17 billion surplus to a $159
billion deficit. Not only have foreign products cornered the
American luxury automobile, home electronic, camera, and
computer-chip markets, but high-tech goods and, hard to
believe, agricultural products are now part of the trade deficit
as well.

Japanese manufacturing workers are now the highest paid
factory workers in the world while U.S. workers are forced
to accept two-tier wage scales and outright pay cuts. All
types of manufacturing continue to dwindle in our country
as a result of outmoded factories and a lack of insight and
interest on the part of American investors. How far has our

position as an industrial power deteriorated? Unfortunately, today more Americans work in fast-food restaurants than in all of manufacturing combined.

Instead of leading the world to new heights, as we did after World War II, we are now pulling it to the edge of a precipice. We have undergone sixteen intense years of economic mismanagement so bad it has made us dependent on loans from other nations and turned us from the world's largest lender to the world's largest borrower almost overnight. Our currency is faltering, and it is harder than ever for the average American to own a home, buy a new car, and pay bills without going deeper into debt.

It is disheartening that fewer products made in the United States are available to American consumers and, worse, that many of the best products are imported. Daily we read about our decline in productivity and our lack of competitiveness and try to understand what has gone wrong. American workers must confront the fact that their wages simply buy less than they did in the early 1970s and that their expenses are higher. At the same time the federal government has gone on a borrowing binge of unmatched proportions that is driving up interest rates, adding to the national debt, and causing alarm in Europe and Japan. And yet, when we listen to the news from the White House, all we hear is that we are somehow more prosperous than ever before.

I would like to believe the stories we hear from Washington that say the economy is getting better, that the October 19, 1987, stock market crash, when more than $1 trillion was lost, was a simple "correction." I would like to believe that Ronald Reagan has been sincere about balancing the budget even though he has added more red ink to our accounts than all previous presidents put together.

But the truth is that we have been bested technologically by the Japanese and that many European countries now enjoy higher standards of living than we do. It may sound discouraging, but it is a fact—and we had better begin planning the next few years cautiously and with our eyes open. The

United States, although still the biggest single economy in the world, is no longer the best or the most competitive and it is far from healthy.

For the last twelve years I have been studying our economy—its structure and how it fits into the larger world economic system. I have consulted with business and government leaders in Europe, Japan, and here at home and have worked with Japanese multinationals like Toyota and with American venture capitalists. While at the United Nations I spearheaded an economic research program called the "Project on the Future," organizing teams of researchers in twenty-one countries to look into the overall economic picture both here and abroad. The conclusion I have drawn from reading through thousands of pages of computer printouts and stacks of research documents is that we must begin to do something now.

Today's economy is faced with real problems. Taken together I call these problems the Decline and Crash of the American economy because they are pulling down our standard of living, threatening our wealth, and weakening our standing in the world, not just in an overnight 508-point collapse of the stock market, but in a slow, steady, unrelenting decline of the economy as a whole. And there is little evidence that the correct steps are being taken—at any level— to end that decline.

This book is not meant to scare, but it is meant to wake people up. Our country is at risk, our investments are in jeopardy, and our future is uncertain. I will show where our problems lie and how they will affect us, and offer a plan to resurrect the United States from its decline. My strategy includes methods on how to preserve individual wealth during these Decline and Crash times. It is my fervent hope that we take the steps that are needed to end the steep decline of our nation so that we can once more assume our position at the helm of the world's economy.

THE DECLINE AND CRASH
OF THE AMERICAN ECONOMY

1

DECLINING WEALTH, INCREASED DEPENDENCE

LET'S go back to the election of 1980. It was in that campaign for the presidency that candidate Ronald Reagan provocatively asked the American people whether we were better or worse off economically, politically, and socially than we were in 1976, the year his opponent Jimmy Carter was elected to the White House by the slimmest of margins. Humiliated abroad by the capturing of the American embassy in Teheran and Carter's aborted rescue attempt, and reeling at home under the enormous weight of soaring inflation, double-digit interest rates, and an uncertain economy, a jittery electorate responded overwhelmingly that we were indeed worse off in 1980. As a consequence Mr. Carter and his family were sent packing, ignored by everyone, including the newly elected Reagan, who never even asked to be briefed by Carter on what had transpired during his term. But if the same question were asked today, how would America answer? Are we better or worse off today than we were in 1984, 1980, 1976, or even 1970? Has our economic slide been arrested?

In one way, we do seem better off; we are certainly a calmer country today than we were during the 1970s. And, under Reagan, it has been rare to see crowds taking to the streets for anything more serious than a parade or neighborhood fair. But in spite of—or perhaps because of—our placidity we have had our share of problems. During the Reagan years the American embassy in Beirut was bombed and, shortly afterward, in another bombing incident, 244 marines were killed as they slept in their barracks at the Beirut airport. In 1981 more than 11,000 air traffic controllers were fired over a pay dispute, causing years of air traffic delays and an overall decrease in air travel safety. We mined Nicaragua's main harbor, which was declared a criminal act by the International Court of Justice in the Hague. We invaded Granada where we learned that even after Reagan's $1.2 trillion defense buildup our competing armed services could not communicate with each other during battle. We attacked Libya and found that some of our closest allies—whose defense we are entrusted with—would not let our war planes take off from our air bases in their countries. Arms and money were sent to the Contras in violation of the Boland Amendment and the Constitution itself. Then, again while they slept, thirty-seven American sailors were killed when one of our "impregnable" guided missile frigates—the *Stark*—was blasted by an Exocet missile from an Iraqi jet as the ship sailed the hostile waters of the Persian Gulf with all of its defenses switched off. And then there was the economy.

Like Frank L. Baum's famous creation, the Wizard of Oz, Ronald Reagan came to Washington during the era of "stagflation," a baggy-pants magician, pockets bulging with dozens of odd-sounding economic tricks. First there was the "magic of the market," which could cure all economic ailments; then the "Laffer curve," which was said to show that cutting taxes would actually raise revenue; followed by the catchall phrase "supply-side economics," which emphasized production, not demand, as the engine that drives economic growth—a theory labeled "backwards" by economists and called "voodoo" by George Bush. From behind the Wizard's screen

Reagan also materialized a rather dubious plan for balancing the federal budget while drastically hiking defense spending and cutting taxes—a trick that first required the transmutation of catsup from a condiment to a vegetable in the nation's school lunch program, followed by Attorney General Meese's assertion that America is a land with no hungry people. Needless to say, the magic fell flat; federal revenue did not increase—but government spending did—and Reagan's budgetary red ink became America's only truly limitless resource.

Just as the wizardry of Reaganomics was taking a weakened, withered American economy and pinning it to the ground, there were those who—in the chaos—hollered their congratulations. "Don't worry, our economy is in transition" we were told as imports of manufactured goods flooded our markets while our own exports all but evaporated. "It's okay, we are moving from a manufacturing economy to an information society" pundits like *Megatrends* author John Naisbitt told us as fewer American companies bothered to produce products in the United States preferring instead to "outsource" everything from Chrysler's Mexican engines to AT& T's phones from Singapore while whole sectors of our economy were lost to the Japanese.

In truth, we have not been moving toward an information society—whatever that bit of Ozian puffery means—nor are we better off today than we were just a decade ago. Instead, as we lose our world dominance in manufacturing, we are also losing millions of high-paying, highly skilled jobs to our overseas competitors, thereby sowing the seeds of our own future impoverishment. But manufacturing is only one casualty in our long decline—a decline stretching back well before the advent of Reaganomics and affecting every sector of the economy and nearly every segment of the population.

For more than a decade and a half—since about 1970— America has been getting poorer as a nation while Americans have been getting poorer as individuals. This terrible fact is proved not only by statistics, but also by observation—we can see the changes in the way we live and the difficulties that confront entire sections of the country. For the average

American, whether single or married, male or female, minority or white, just making a decent living—with income and buying power rising faster than personal debt—is getting harder each year; the good life in America, for the first time in our history, is increasingly beyond the reach of all but a few.

The difficulties confronting us are not limited to the homeless and hungry, who now number in the millions and are offered so little—by the standards of the rest of the advanced world—in the form of help. Increasingly, the middle class, the mainstay of the economy, is being squeezed—shrinking, in fact, as thousands of individuals, both working and unemployed, join the ranks of the "newly poor," one of the surest signs of this nation's decline.

To live like Americans did in the 1950s and 1960s, when we were the envy of the world, now usually requires two wage earners in each household owing to the fact that American wages, income, and buying power have actually fallen since the early 1970s. This may come as a surprise to Wall Street tycoons like Michael Milken, who earned $80 million in commissions in 1986 selling "junk bonds," to raise money for corporate takeovers, or to the heads of some of our manufacturing companies, like Chrysler's Lee Iacocca, who earned $20 million from a company bailed out by the government just a few years earlier, or to the leaders of the defense establishment, like Northrop's T. V. Jones, who earned $1.1 million selling weapons to the government, or to bankers like Citibank's John Reed, who earned $1.1 million from a bank that granted billions of dollars in bad loans to Brazil. But to tens of millions of Americans the era of decreasing incomes is a painful and unavoidable fact. According to the U.S. Congress's Joint Economic Committee (JEC), which monitors and reports on the major economic trends in this country, the earnings of the average thirty-year-old worker—when corrected for inflation and converted into today's dollar terms—have plummeted from a before-taxes high of $25,253 in 1973 to only $18,763 in 1987, a decline of nearly 25 percent. Workers in other age categories have experienced similar drops in earnings while at the same time the prices of such basic necessities as housing, food, day-care services, transportation, and medical care have more than quadrupled since the beginning of the 1970s. Rising prices and falling wages have made life much harder for the average American and, despite all the talk in Congress of restoring American drive and competitiveness, there is no end in sight for this most destructive downward trend.

There is, of course, the counterargument that American wages are currently too high and that their decline is to be welcomed if we are to be competitive internationally. After all, the argument goes, as American wages tumble, the cost of producing goods at home will also decrease, enabling U.S. companies both to export more and to compete more favorably at home against imported goods. This is the point of view taken by many of the conservative economists advising the Reagan administration and, on the surface, it seems to make some sense.

But there are a number of problems with the argument. First, if we continue on the path of converting America into a low-wage nation so as to make ourselves more competitive, where do we stop? The average Mexican wage is a little more than $2,000 per year for workers fabricating parts for Ford and Chrysler along the U.S.-Mexican border. The typical Korean working on the Hyundai automobile assembly line makes a little more than $3,000 annually, while the Brazilian workers who hammer together the Mercury Tracer and the Volkswagen Fox make about $2,400 per year. Must we lower our wages and our standard of living to these levels in order to compete? Of course not. But we do have to ensure that the American worker is vastly more productive than his overseas counterparts and that American industry is more efficient than that of any other nation.

From World War I until the early 1970s American companies had higher productivity and greater efficiency and so were able to pay their workers more than those in other countries while still dominating world business and turning in record profits. And these high rates of productivity and efficiency kept us growing at tremendous rates of speed, giving us the economic clout to enter new markets in countries around the world. The situation is no different today. As long as we are the most productive and efficient country then we can also be the country with the highest wages. But productivity and efficiency have as much to do with the management, investment, planning, and research practices of our companies as they do with the wages and quality of work of our individual workers.

It is important for the United States to remain a high-wage country because high-wage workers have greater buying power. Well-paid workers spending their salary checks stimulate the economy. If these workers spend their paychecks on American goods and services they will keep their colleagues around the country busy and employed. If they instead choose to save their money, then the banks will have plenty of money to loan. High wages help prime the economic pump—something Henry Ford learned firsthand when Ford reluctantly raised his workers' wages to the astronomical sum of $1 per day, just prior to the First World War. Instead of bankrupting the company he found that his workers suddenly had enough money to buy some of the cars they produced.

As long as our workers produce efficiently and can buy American products their high wages aid the economy. But when there are few American-made products to choose from, then those high wages only help to stimulate the economy of some other country. If U.S. wages fall, however, our buying power also falls and ultimately the U.S. economy must slow down.

Few recent developments are of such a cataclysmic nature as this real and observable erosion of individual buying power and of national wealth. The decline is accompanied not only by a significant deterioration in our standard of living but by an erosion in our standing as a world power and in our ability to influence events. In international relations, just as in local and national politics, wealth is the surest measure of power and, short of war, the final arbiter of any dispute. It is not our superior ethical behavior that has given us superpower status and the vast privileges that go with it, but our singular ability to "bear any burden" and "pay any price," as John F. Kennedy said. To bear those burdens and pay those prices our industries must be competitive and our workers' incomes must remain high. The United States, as a whole, must be flourishing so that our leadership comes not as a sacrifice, as in the Soviet Union, but as one of the rewards of our capacity to generate wealth efficiently and intelligently. It was the capacity to generate wealth that enabled us to dictate the terms of peace after the Second World War; rebuild Europe in a more peaceful and prosperous form; keep open sea lanes in such diverse locales as the Horn of Africa, the northern Atlantic, and the Bering Sea; check the expansion of the Soviet Union; and broker a peace treaty between Egypt and Israel that is favorable to our interests. If Americans earn too little to pay the price of global leadership, who will? And how will they treat us?

For nearly seventeen years now we have been doggedly pursued by the same downward spiral Reagan so clearly identified in 1980. We have been losing ground in a sharp Decline and Crash of enormous magnitude, shaking us from prosperity and from the summit of achievement, tarnishing our image in the world, putting our children's futures at risk, and making our nation dependent on the largesse of others.

How have we become dependent? Let's take just one example, the explosive and inflationary growth of the federal budget. Despite years of easy talk about cutting federal spending that has come from behind the Wizard's screen at the White House and in spite of Congress's Gramm-Rudman Amendment and its semi-tough stance on limiting spending, the federal budget has still managed to more than triple between 1975 and 1987. In 1987 alone, the federal deficit grew by $173.2 billion and, to continue paying for its programs in areas like health and human services, education, road construction, national defense, AIDS research, foreign assistance, and the space program, to name but a few, the government is forced to borrow sums equal to that deficit. But Americans are no longer rich enough to loan such large sums to the government by buying bonds and Treasury notes. After taking care of our own expenses in an ever more hostile economy, we just don't have enough cash. So, just to keep in business, the government must go to foreign lenders to borrow the sums needed to pay for that deficit. Who are the lenders? In 1987, the Japanese loaned our government enough money to cover about 40 percent of the $173.2 billion deficit while another 10 to 20 percent came from the Europeans. If it weren't for those rich Europeans, and those richer Japanese, our government would have had to shut down—or raise taxes.

But creditors who loan that much money to us are not likely to sit idly by if our government makes a decision they feel not to be in their own best interests; they can put pressure on us in many subtle and not so subtle ways in return for those vital loans, thereby weakening our position of leadership in the world. This erosion of leadership was demonstrated most graphically during the 1987 summit meeting of heads of state in Venice when none of the U.S. initiatives urging our allies to stimulate their economies and to help end the war in the Persian Gulf gained more than verbal support. The international press promptly carried stories about the United States' lost influence over its allies owing to its mismanagement of the economy and its new status as the world's biggest borrower. The United States' loss of influence at Venice was so great that Reagan was not able to convince our allies to join the effort to protect Persian Gulf shipping even though that area accounts for less than 4 percent of our own oil imports but much more than half of the oil imported by Europe and Japan. The unwritten story may just be that we are now forced to risk—and lose—American lives protecting European and Japanese oil imports in exchange for their loans to cover our deficit. A small amount of help in the Persian Gulf came only months after the summit concluded when it became obvious we could not do the job alone.

Before 1986, when we were the world's largest creditor instead of the world's largest debtor, we demanded concessions from those countries that were in debt to us. Amid loud protests, we routinely forced countries like Turkey, Israel, Mexico, Brazil, and a host of others to change their economic and sometimes even political structures in order to qualify for more loans from our government. In many instances we dabbled in the internal affairs of those countries by requiring them to alter the value of their currencies, decontrol farm prices, and shift their investment priorities—with varying degrees of success—in exchange for cash. Israel may be the best example of this: In 1985 Herbert Stein, Gerald Ford's chief economist, was sent by the Reagan administration to Jerusalem to help the Israeli government cut its spending plans in exchange for more of our money. The Israeli government of Shimon Peres—a socialist with an economic perspective far different from Reagan's—had to agree because without our help they would have gone bankrupt. Now that nearly 20 percent of our own annual federal budget is funded not by taxes but by borrowing, and with more than half of that coming from overseas, we must ask ourselves if we will not someday soon be seeing a Japanese or European economist appointed to oversee all major American economic decisions as a prerequisite for more cash infusions from abroad.

IN SPITE OF all that borrowing our lives have not gotten any better, nor has the economy really grown. We have not been borrowing to increase our productivity or to finance economic expansion but instead just to stem the decline. In world terms we have slipped from an undisputed first place in standard of living achieved during the 1950s and 1960s to fourteenth today. Other critical indicators such as infant mortality, average life span, access to medical care, and overall adult literacy trail countries like Sweden, Switzerland, Norway, and Germany because we are no longer creating enough wealth to provide for all of our citizens. We may still cast a giant shadow, but like most things in the land of Oz, it is done with mirrors.

Part of the decline results from the fact that in industry after industry—and in the services, too—we are being over-

taken not just by the Japanese, but also by the small and
medium-sized countries of Europe and the newly emerging
countries of Asia. The number one country for banking services, insurance, stock brokering, semiconductor production,
automobile manufacturing, robot production, consumer electronic manufacturing, and the very vital and strategic machine
tool industry is no longer the United States but Japan. Japan,
once derided as a "copycat nation" unable to lead or innovate,
now is at the forefront of research in areas that will dominate
the economy of tomorrow, for example, high-strength ceramics for automobile and airplane engines, supercomputers, fiber
optics, and fermentation. And the Europeans are gaining on
our lead in passenger aircraft production, in space research,
and in telecommunications and are overtaking us in advertising, banking, and engineering services. The Soviet Union has
again soared ahead of us in its space program with the introduction of new heavy lift booster rockets capable of lifting
tremendous payloads into space. Korea and Brazil make
cheaper, and often better, steel than we do and have all but
taken over the textile industry. Our shipbuilding industry—
the same industry that built tens of thousands of "Liberty"
ships during the four short years of our involvement in World
War II—languishes while devastated Japan has become the
world's largest builder of supertankers and freighters.

Whole sectors of the vast American market have been
abandoned by U.S. firms without even a fight so that even
if you wanted to, you could not buy an American-made VCR,
camcorder, compact-disc player, fax machine, digital tape
cassette recorder, mini television receiver, "Walkman," digital
television, or quality 35-mm camera. You would also have
a hard time purchasing a shirt, suit, or any other piece of
wearing apparel made completely in the United States—the
law allows clothing to be labeled "Made in America" even
if everything is really made elsewhere save for a few final
stitches sewn here. The same goes for a fast-food hamburger
patty—the beef comes from Mexico, Argentina, or even as
far away as Australia. And with automobiles, it is increasingly
difficult to find a truly "American" car—that is, one assembled

domestically with less than 20 percent of its component parts imported from Mexico, Japan, Korea, Taiwan, or Brazil. In short, in less than twenty years we have lost our commanding position not in just one industry, but in dozens, all without a fight.

To have gone from the world's dominant industrial power to the world's greatest importer of industrial goods in such a short span of time is nearly incomprehensible. Without shame or protest we have witnessed cities laid to waste by the wholesale destruction of some of our most basic industries. Families in Detroit, Gary, Pittsburgh, and Cleveland have seen firsthand the deterioration of the industries their fathers and grandfathers built, and the casual abandonment of some of the most experienced workers in the world—workers that the Japanese and many of the Europeans would retrain, but never fire. As I mentioned in the introduction, consider just one statistic that shows how far we have fallen: In America today, there are more people working in fast-food restaurants than in all of the manufacturing industries combined.

These changes do not mean that America is transforming itself into an "information society," as we shall see. Few programs exist to train industrial workers to become high-quality information workers. These programs, like CETA— the Comprehensive Employment and Training Act—were among the first casualties of the Reagan years. Rather, it means that America is sliding down the wage ladder from high-paying, highly productive manufacturing jobs to low-paying, low-productivity service jobs. While we were dreaming of becoming the "Affluent Society," which as early as the late 1960s John Kenneth Galbraith said we were destined to become, we were in reality on our way to becoming the "Minimum-Wage Society" with armies of underpaid service workers earning less than they did the previous decade and having fewer hopes for the future than their parents had.

In spite of this fall from wealth there have been far too few cries of "emergency." Perhaps we have simply been lulled into complacency by the lumbering pace of the Decline and Crash. Perhaps the bigger numbers that decorate our paychecks, but actually buy less in the stores, have hypnotized us into believing that we are not in fact on a downward path. Or maybe the real magic of Reaganomics has been to blind us to the truth of our decline. After all, how could a president we admire so much and who has spoken out so beautifully and for so long about economic growth have actually allowed our economic contraction to continue? A contraction that began during the first term of Richard M. Nixon with danger signals observable at every point along the way?

If these were different times, and if our long economic decline had occurred more rapidly, surely we would have taken action. Had anyone been listening, the October 19 Stock Market Crash should have sounded the alarm. A government concerned about the $1 trillion decline in stock prices in just one week, or about the overall 14 percent decline in incomes since 1970 and frightened by our loss of industrial leadership, might have convened a brain trust of wise men and women and established a national plan for renewal. This, after all, is what the Japanese did so successfully, when they identified which American-dominated industries they wanted to control after the war, fixed those industries in their sights, and then picked off some of our best companies one by one. And a national plan for economic growth is what we require of most of the emerging nations we help before we will grant them aid. The French have made great strides by devising a national plan and so have the Swedes, Germans, and Koreans. Yet we have been extremely reluctant to devise such a plan, in spite of the fact that nearly every nation that has taken that action has surpassed us in level of growth. Instead, in our dubious wisdom, we have relied upon the wizardry of Reaganomics and the "voodoo" of the market. We have labeled planning much too "political" and allowed our companies and their managers to systematically relocate most of their manufacturing facilities far from our shores. Instead of planning, we have relied on the spirit of laissez-faire and what Adam Smith, in his eighteenth-century wisdom, called the "invisible hand." Unfortunately, the invisible hand has so far given only invisible results.

To those Americans who participated directly in the great economic expansion that immediately followed World War II and lasted into the late 1960s, the revelation that Americans as a group have been getting poorer since the early 1970s may come as quite a shock. After all, those who were young adults just after the war came of age when there was a shortage of workers and a surplus of jobs. They participated in an American economy that was functioning at its optimum; they knew a dynamic engine that astounded the world with its productivity and creativity and invented whole new technologies, industries, and ways of living. Transistors, computers, automation, integrated circuits, trips to the moon, biotechnology, jumbo jets, green cities built in the desert, plastics, automated agriculture, robots, credit cards, and many other innovations flowed freely from America's creative cornucopia. As the French social commentator Jean-Jacques Servan-Schrieber wrote in the late 1960s, America's dynamism had challenged the world and had created entirely new ways of solving problems free from the confines of history, ideology, and religion. In short, America had chosen a path for its own development that knew no limits, tolerated no bounds, and to which other nations could only aspire.

Even without going to the moon themselves, that first post–World War II generation lived very well, imbued with a sense of optimism about a future that seemed filled with ever-expanding possibilities. They grew accustomed to rapidly increasing wages, low university tuitions, and full scholarships for every G.I. And they grew accustomed to growth. These Americans also learned how to save and were able to put away at least twelve cents for every dollar earned, filling up the banking system with money that could be loaned at modest rates. They could easily afford to own their own homes—mortgage interest rates were between 2 and 4 percent while inflation was practically nil—and feel a sense of pride behind the wheel of a Chevrolet or Oldsmobile, the world's most popular, powerful, and best-built cars. These Americans were members of one of the world's most fortunate and upwardly mobile generations—a group that watched with amusement as touring groups of Japanese businessmen visited our factories, department stores, and shops—instead of our vacation spots—photographing the countless details needed to support the American Dream financially and industrially.

To subsequent generations, those of us who came of age during the sixties, seventies, and eighties, the news of our country's decline is one of the more painful facts of life. These Americans have firsthand knowledge of plant closings, mortgages yo-yoing between 8 and 22 percent, American brand names being placed on imported goods of every kind, and annual university tuitions that nearly equal a full year's pay. To them, America is not a land of ever-expanding possibilities but a country of disillusionment, decline, and frustration, a country whose leading labor unions no longer negotiate salary increases but wage "givebacks" in a desperate effort to keep the last remnants of our industrial workers employed in what are now some of the world's most out-of-date factories. For these Americans—baby boomers and younger—even their parents' savings habits are impossible to duplicate. For them banks are no longer places for keeping money safe and accruing interest, but for obtaining credit cards and loans to maintain what crumbs they have managed to glean from the American Dream.

By 1980, America's decline became nearly universal and it was in that year that the American Dream was dealt a mighty blow. Until 1980 the percentage of Americans owning their own homes was on the rise following an upward trend that began after World War II and lasted for more than thirty years. Since 1980 the percentage of Americans owning their own homes has been on the decline, not because older people are selling off their property and relocating to retirement complexes in Florida or Arizona, but because young families, earning less than they once did, can no longer afford to buy.

Home ownership is probably the single most important element in the American Dream. It represents by far the largest share of most families' wealth and provides them with far more than shelter. It is also a store of value that can be borrowed against, to pay for a child's college education, or sold to provide money for retirement. Perhaps most important, owning a home is also the most powerful symbol for Americans of having become full participants in the life of the country.

But the economy of the country has grown too weak to support individual home ownership the way it once did. Consider how much more it now costs to own a home than it did during our boom years. According to the Bureau of Labor Statistics, the average thirty-year-old head of household in 1949 had to spend just 14 percent of a paycheck to make the payments on a home. In 1949, with such low monthly mortgage payments, the average family needed only one wage earner and there was still plenty left over at the end of the month to enjoy some of the other pleasures of the American Dream. By 1970 the same average thirty-year-old head of household had to spend more than 21 percent of a paycheck to pay for that home—a somewhat larger share than was comfortable, but still small enough so that one wage earner could support a family and a home and still have a little money left to save. By 1986 the cost of home ownership had soared, consuming more than 44 percent of the average thirty-year-old's paycheck. For the average younger family of today, one wage earner is no longer sufficient to support home ownership. Yet, even with two wage earners, today's home owners still have less money left over at the end of each billing cycle than did those one-income families of 1970.

Two alarming facts illustrate the difficulties today's new home owner must face: First, current mortgage initiation fees alone are now larger than the average down payments on homes purchased in the late 1950s and early 1960s. Second, since 1970, the average price of a home in the United States has increased more than 400 percent while the price of a home near our major cities has increased even more.

You don't have to go far to confirm the facts of our decline. The seacoast town in Connecticut where I live is a case in point. It is a pleasant place with black-and-white New England-style homes nestled along miles of beach, within easy commuting distance of New York. However, with home prices skyrocketing after more than fifteen years of inflation, and interest rates not far from the double digits, few young families can afford to move into this town. As a result, like so many other suburbs, schools are closing, teachers are leaving, and the population is shifting toward the mature end of the age spectrum, to say the least.

It is not just the cost of buying homes that has risen; rents, too, have increased as landlords have been forced to pay more for their apartment buildings owing to inflation. Changes in the tax laws are also boosting rental prices by forcing landlords to charge their tenants more to compensate for the loss of certain deductions. The increased financial pressure put on renters has made it harder for them to save the money needed for a down payment on their own home.

With renting becoming a way of life in America, many millions of people will never have the opportunity to accumulate tangible wealth. Without real estate assets to sell at retirement, a steadily increasing number of Americans are destined to become dependent on Social Security as their sole means of support during their later years. This paints a grim picture for the future, especially for the baby boomers who make up the single largest segment of the population. When this large group of individuals finally makes it to retirement with few financial assets and little real wealth, it will merely confirm the breadth of the economy's fall.

We have compensated for the increased costs of living in America by sacrificing savings and going deeper into debt. The average Japanese now saves about 22 percent of each growing paycheck, while the average American is able to save only between 2 and 4 percent of a shrinking one. For America this level of savings is clearly insufficient to meet our needs and is one reason why we must borrow from abroad to support the federal deficit.

These figures regarding savings, though, are somewhat misleading because in the United States it is the older generation that is doing most of the saving. Younger Americans—even the so-called yuppies—just do not earn enough to put any money in the bank. These younger Americans have become what economists call "net dissavers" because they consistently spend more than they earn. To pay for their purchases these young dissavers are using every form of consumer credit imaginable—installment credit, multiple credit cards, department store credit, second mortgages (if they are lucky enough to own a house), credit and rebates from manufacturers, and on and on. In fact, banks have been very creative in making credit available. Centralized data bases, like the one TRW maintains, can cut the time it takes to have a loan approved from days to minutes. Even with big-ticket items, like cars, stereos, quality cameras, and computers, loan approval can take less than a day. Automated bank computers routinely scan the data bases for new clients and send out notices pre-approving these potential applicants for additional credit.

These highly efficient techniques have worked marvelously for those companies that supply consumer credit. The only problem is that, though all this consumer debt may serve as a stimulus to today's economy by boosting buying power, it also serves as a drag on tomorrow's economy as interest payments consume more and more of each debtor's income. And with debt growing faster than income it is not inconceivable that the brake on future growth will come abruptly, as abruptly as the market crash of 1987.

But who can blame these youthful borrowers for dipping deeper into the credit troughs? After all, they are just trying to live at least the way their parents did, when money was plentiful, jobs abundant, and growth robust. They are borrowing to finance the American Dream, and in ordinary times this spending spree would keep our factories humming twenty-four hours a day. In today's Decline and Crash economy, with so many of the goods we buy originating outside the United States, the accumulation of debt serves only to keep the fires of industry burning brightly overseas. Selling to the United States, as our economy collapses, is just the stimulus many countries need to propel themselves upward in the ranks of development. And what do they buy from us as we fall deeper into the red and as the value of the dollar tumbles? They buy our Treasury notes, our stocks and bonds, our real estate, our factories, farms, and mines. They buy our computer and software companies and our skyscrapers as well. They buy, with their profits, large chunks of our future and with it huge reserves of influence. But one thing is for sure: They do not buy our products—those few remaining for purchase. Such is the legacy of Reaganomics and the policies of the past.

2

THE MYTH OF
THE INFORMATION
ECONOMY

ALTHOUGH there have been many economic gurus who have heralded new ages in America, in the last decade or two few of those ages have lived up to their promise and few have been as potentially damaging to the fabric of the country as the so-called "Information Age." The Atomic Age didn't produce free electricity; the Computer Age still has its share of illiterates; the Automobile Age still hasn't given us those automated cars that can whisk three passengers down the highway while the driver joins them in a hand of bridge; the Space Age hasn't produced a permanent space station or a manned trip to Mars; and the Age of Aquarius has given way to the Aquisitions Age. What about the Information Age?

The principal balladeer of the Age of Information is the bearded former insurance executive John Naisbitt, author of the hugely successful but shallow book *Megatrends*. According to Naisbitt, whose research consists of clipping articles from small-town newspapers around the country, information and manufacturing are wholly separate domains. Information itself is an engine of economic growth and the manipulation of information will someday provide for all of our needs. In Naisbitt's view the deindustrialization of America and the rise of the Information Age are positive and will usher in an era during which we will enjoy both high technology and the added plus of a higher level of sensuality owing to increased leisure time.

Naisbitt doesn't tell us, though, where all that high technology will be made. This is important since we are rapidly losing our lead in high tech, as evidenced by the fact that the government has decided to restrict the imports of Japanese chips into the United States while our own producers use the import restraints to—you guessed it—"become more competitive." It is interesting to note that many of the products coming into this country from Japan are made there under special licensing agreements from the same American manufacturers that are now begging for the government's help.

Naisbitt's "high tech, high touch" is a catchy phrase but one must wonder if it is really the kind of future we want. So far, the recent big boom in the service/information economy is based on all the new jobs created in the consumer and retail sales fields—specifically fast food, health care, and business-related office services. These three areas of the economy are responsible for 40 percent of the new jobs that have been created during the Reagan era. Without arguing that there is a causal link between the growth in fast-food establishments and the growth in the need for health-care services (health care now accounts for more than 10 percent of the economy, yet Americans are only sixteenth in the world in life span and infant mortality among blacks in the United States is worse than in some third world countries), it is interesting to note that most of the workers in these growing areas are working for close to minimum wage. According to the liberal labor economist Emma Rothschild, employment in health care, business services, and fast foods combined now exceeds employment in all of the basic production industries in the United States: construction, all machinery, all electric and electronic equipment, motor vehicles, aircraft, shipbuilding, all chemicals and related products, and all scientific and technical instrument production. Frying hamburgers may be a more sensuous experience (high touch) than building airplanes or trucks, but hamburgers are quickly consumed whereas each truck and airplane produced generates wealth and jobs for years.

When getting down to the specifics of the information sector, *Megatrends* author Naisbitt mentioned two companies as being among his favorites in the Age of Information. One was Apple Computer, which despite recent growth has closed three plants, eased out its founder, laid off 2,400 employees, and failed to introduce a new, successful product in three years. All this just after having won Naisbitt's praise. AT&T, Naisbitt's other favorite, laid off 24,000 workers after its breakup when the federal government found the company to be in violation of anti-trust laws, and shifted its consumer products production from the United States to Singapore. Not only did AT&T lay off thousands of workers, as part of its anti-trust settlement it was also forced to divest itself of its local telephone companies and its research lab. In fact, the entire information sector of the economy is in a deep slump with even giants like IBM, Wang, and NCR showing only slight positive earnings and many of the companies at the farthest reaches of technology going out of business entirely. And don't forget our high-tech trade deficit with the rest of the world as we are inundated with clones of IBM PCs and with boatloads of VCRs, stereos, televisions, cameras, and other consumer electronics products—a market we invented and once dominated and have since lost.

Why is the high-tech/information sector faltering? According to John Akers, president of IBM, high tech is faltering because capital spending by business—the kind of spending that directly translates into productivity and manufacturing capacity gains—continues to be sluggish. In other words, much of the high-tech, information, and service sectors' fortunes rest on how well the other parts of the economy perform, especially manufacturing.

The information and service sectors often follow the economy, rather than lead it. By following economic trends, the success of these sectors is thus dependent on the success of the productive sectors. This means there is no clear break between the "information sector" and the rest of the economy. True, information and intellectual inputs can be specified and even measured, but they do not exist in a vacuum. Without manufacturing applications, engineers are as unemployable as lathe and milling machine operators. And, during the fifteen years of this Decline and Crash, the demand for high-quality scientific, technical, and business information has not increased sufficiently to pull the nation out of its slump, nor has it contributed to increasing the productivity of the growing services sector of the economy.

This interrelationship between the sectors is not confined simply to information and manufacturing. Services, too, are intimately tied to the other parts of the economy. Fast-food restaurants live or die depending on the total employment picture in a given area, as do day-care centers and shopping malls. When high-wage manufacturing is booming, it spills over to the other sectors of the economy and creates prosperity all around. Marion, Ohio, where Honda motorcycles and cars are assembled, is booming—and not just at the factory. The clothing stores, restaurants, and other service sector businesses in Marion are growing as a result of the high-wage jobs brought to that community by the Japanese manufacturing plant. Without those high-wage jobs, Marion would be in the same economic doldrums as the rest of the Midwest.

Another real problem with Naisbitt's analysis is that it does not look at the whole picture, not even at the most basic statistics regarding our trade problems. These statistics show that, aside from oil, the greatest portion of our balance-of-trade deficit results from our gigantic imports of manufactured goods, such as machinery and electronics components, and our slipping exports of products in these same categories. To ignore trade, as Naisbitt has, means to look at the United States as if it were a self-contained island instead of a dynamic nation constantly interacting with the rest of the world. The majority of our trade problems have nothing to do with information or services but with the fact that our exports of manufactured goods are declining relative to our imports of those same goods. Our exports of information and of services, everything from software to engineering consultancies, in no way make up for our imports of machines and electronic components. In fact, today the only thing that we export more of than we import is raw materials. We have recently even become a net importer of food—while our farmers are going out of business. It is highly unlikely that these tremendous imports can be offset by selling software, publishing magazines, and selling insurance policies abroad, as Naisbitt suggests. Actually, as we shift even more into producing "high-tech, high-touch" services and information products, our situation worsens.

Imagine the implications of taking Naisbitt's theory one step further. For instance, if we were to decrease the amount of manufacturing that takes place in our economy, we would be decreasing our biggest export item, and we would also have to import more manufactured goods from abroad. Consider what would happen if we stopped selling tractors, cranes, computers, trucks, and telecommunications equipment abroad while at the same time we imported more of those goods. The impact upon the economy would be horrendous. First, our imports of manufactured goods, about $282.1 billion in 1986, would rise even higher while our exports of those goods, about $148.7 billion during the same period, would collapse. The net result of the "high-tech, high-touch" society would be trade gaps many times greater than those of today.

Naisbitt's idea is to transform America into a services and information economy, which means, presumably, that our export losses from abandoning manufacturing would be made up by our increased exports of services and intellectual property, such as new patents. Suddenly, we would flood the world's markets with our superior banking services, computer software, records, books, and movie cassettes. Yet even if taken all together, these service and information exports would offset just a small percentage of our manufacturing losses. Moreover, information and services are subject to intense competition from abroad. Unlike tangible goods, services need to be very precisely matched to the market. For instance, selling information products and services abroad means taking into account differences not only in culture and language, but also in accounting practices, currencies, and professional standards. Engineering and safety standards vary in different countries and professional licenses are not always recognized abroad. All of this means that boosting our exports of services to offset greater imports of manufactured products would entail a tremendous effort on our part, and it would be practically impossible to raise this component of the economy so that it is large enough to offset *all* of our merchandise imports. In short, Naisbitt's notion of transforming America into a high-tech, high-touch society would only accelerate our Decline and Crash.

The information and service sectors are more intimately connected, and dependent, on manufacturing than most futurists are prepared to admit. Professors Stephen S. Cohen and John Zysman, of the University of California at Berkeley, have studied the links between the manufacturing and the information/service sectors in depth. Their analysis, called *Manufacturing Matters* (New York: Basic Books, 1987), brings to light how dependent the information and service sectors are on the health of our manufacturing industries.

According to Cohen and Zysman, a large portion of the jobs in the U.S. service and information sector are "tightly" linked to manufacturing. Generally, most economists figure that today about 20 percent of the American work force is engaged in manufacturing—down from 33 percent in the booming 1950s. But if those direct, tight linkages between the service and manufacturing sectors are taken into account, then the percentage of Americans whose livelihoods depend on the health of the manufacturing sector is actually much higher. Although difficult to estimate with complete certainty, Cohen and Zysman write that "we would have to say that the particular organizational structure of manufacturing production in the United States (and probably in most other highly advanced economies) makes the employment of perhaps 40 or even 50 or even 60 million Americans, half to two-thirds or even three-quarters of whom are conventionally counted as service workers, depend directly upon manufacturing production. 'Depend' is used to mean that if manufacturing goes, those jobs go with it." In other words, half of all jobs in America exist only because we are still a manufacturing nation.

The concept of economic "sectors" as discrete entities is very fuzzy. Take, for example, the "agricultural sector." Americans are very proud that only about 3 to 4 percent of the work force is employed in agriculture. Having so few people produce so much food is a mark of our development. With no more than about 3 million farmers, ranch hands, grain silo operators, millers, fence menders, and cowboys, we produce enough to feed half the world.

But what about those service/information sector workers whose livelihoods are directly dependent on agriculture? If agriculture moved offshore, and we started importing all of our food from Mexico, a great deal more than 3 to 4 percent of the work force would be affected. For example, according to Cohen and Zysman, crop dusters, truckers, and large animal veterinarians are directly dependent on the agricultural sector but are not counted in its statistics. So are farm insurance agents, government farm extension officers, corporate and university plant geneticists, farm credit officers, pharmaceutical research scientists, tractor manufacturers, agricultural publishers, and so on.

If we were to get out of agriculture—the way we are told to get out of manufacturing—nearly all of these people whose futures are linked directly to this sector would lose their jobs. How many people would that be? According to the U.S. Department of Agriculture, the work of as many as 28.4 million Americans is directly dependent on agriculture— more than a quarter of the total work force. Cohen and Zysman think the Department of Agriculture's figures are much too high, yet their much more conservative estimate still links the livelihoods of 6 to 8 million American job holders directly to agriculture. According to Cohen and Zysman, these men and women are not counted as members of the agricultural sector but nevertheless should be considered "part of direct farm production." If they are correct, then the agricultural sector is directly responsible for the employment of between 6 and 8 percent of the total American work force—double those normally counted as belonging to the agriculture sector. If the Department of Agriculture is correct in its accounting, the number of jobs dependent on a healthy agricultural sector is even greater.

The same is true with respect to manufacturing. If we were to ship our remaining manufacturing companies offshore, consider the number of design engineers, consultants, maintenance workers, truckers, software publishers, university researchers, specialized insurers, financial planners, safety experts, waste-disposal technicians, and others who would suddenly be out of work. Using their concept of linkage, Cohen and Zysman estimate that fully 47 percent of the total American work force is engaged in the production of goods, which means that almost half of all information/service sector jobs are directly tied to our capability to produce goods. For these members of the so-called "Information Age" the further loss of America's manufacturing capacity would spell disaster; nearly half of all our jobs would be lost. This is quite different from the picture Naisbitt paints.

Consider semiconductors. If we were to fail to regain our lead in semiconductors, and allow our chip-making industries to go offshore, we would also very rapidly lose our edge in the other technologies linked to that industry. Suddenly there would be no domestic demand for high-tech mask making, assembly clean rooms, specialized design equipment, chip foundries, and other vital components of the semiconductor industry. With the loss of these related industries others would disappear, and there would be generally the same diminishing effect throughout the economy.

If in a few years we decided to manufacture chips again, the price for entering a market we had abandoned would be prohibitive because of the amount of innovations and new developments. Apple Computer may have started on a kitchen table a decade ago with a few thousand dollars in start-up capital, but today the capital required to enter that same market is in the tens of millions of dollars. Companies that missed or abandoned that particular market are unlikely to attempt to enter it again. The rule is that it costs many times more to enter a mature manufacturing field than it does to enter a field at its inception.

Aside from the superstars of the service and information sectors, such as rock musicians, doctors, lawyers, basketball players, engineers, and airline pilots, the average service worker's salary is on the low end of the scale. The more service workers we have, the faster we will become a low-wage country. According to the Department of Commerce, the salary of a service worker in a retail trade is a little less than half that of a worker in a manufacturing job—$394.23 per week for manufacturing versus $174.60 per week for retail—and both earn less than those employed in the construction industry, who average $462.02 per week. According to the Joint Economic Committee, of the 9 million new jobs created between 1979 and 1985—primarily service sector jobs—44 percent were paid $7,000 or less per year, $134.62 per week, which is less than the current average for retail workers. That is because productivity in services is growing even less rapidly (and is declining in some areas such as office services) than it is in the production sector of the economy, with each increase in productivity won only with difficulty and often at great expense. Moving workers from production jobs in such prematurely dying industries as steelmaking to jobs in the low-paying but growing service sector means considerable expense in retraining for a lower paying job, which engenders considerable resentment, and just plain bad service, as hard-pressed families endure further cuts in their standards of living as payment for their membership in the "Information Age."

It is important to remember what is happening to our steelmaking industry. In the fifties and sixties the United States led the world in total steel production using the most modern technology available. Today the United States uses outmoded technology and steel production has decreased drastically; only 40 percent of U.S. steel is produced by the technologically superior continuous casting method, far below the average in Japan, Korea, and even Brazil. USX, the new name for United State Steel, is an industrial fossil that utilizes continuous casting technology to produce only 26 percent of its steel; even third world producers have plants more modern than USX's. As a result of using outmoded technology that prevents the U.S. steel industry from competing with those modern foreign producers, the size of the entire work force has shrunk from 700,000 in 1978 to fewer than 140,000 in 1987. The industry as a whole lost $8 billion over the last four years. The only way U.S. steel production maintains any significant market share is because our government limits imports.

When steel mills close down, the livelihoods of towns and cities are greatly affected. In such a depressed economy it is unlikely that a small steelmaking town can support growth in the service sector. And what about the billions of dollars spent by preceding generations on the infrastructure of the steel industry—railroads, waterways, electric power plants and grids—and of the billions spent on other dying industries as well? Do we just write that off, as the leaders of the steel industry are now doing? And what of the years of experience accumulated by the laid-off workers? Do we simply consign that experience to the ash can of history as we choose not to modernize and compete? What has our much-touted information revolution done for this most basic of industries?

Futurists should realize that the emerging leaders in the services and information sectors of the economy will be no more immune from competition than were their predecessors. It is both arrogant and self-defeating to think that we can maintain our lead in services any better than we did in manufacturing unless a radically different course is taken.

As a matter of fact, there already is competition from abroad in the information and services sectors. For U.S. engineers in the high-tech end of the service economy who design and plan new products to be manufactured offshore in Korea or Taiwan, the future is not as rosy as we might at first imagine. Professors Cohen and Zysman and others argue that designing a product today is not enough; to be truly up-to-date, engineers must be intimately familiar with the rapidly changing production environment or they will not be able to take advantage of quickly advancing technology. But designers working at their design stations in the United States will not always be privy to what happens when their parts are built on the shop floors of Taiwan or South Korea. Production information will not be fed back to the United States but will stay instead with the engineers in Taiwan or Korea, enabling them to gain valuable design and manufacturing insights and to leapfrog American engineers.

Without knowledge of what happens on the shop floor, American engineers will fall behind and our information inputs will diminish. Cohen and Zysman argue that if the manufacturing sector continues to go offshore, ultimately it will take engineering and the other vital high-tech services with it, further weakening the structure of our economy.

The same is true with services. With the factories gone, and with a growing loss of knowledge about factory production processes, it is not very likely that an American engineer will be in demand by South Korean, Taiwanese, and Japanese electronics manufacturers.

The jobs exodus in the information sector has already begun in some key industries. The giant San Francisco-based Bechtel Corporation uses engineers in Taiwan to design some of its most complicated civil engineering projects; American Express now has much of its data processing done offshore in the Caribbean; Indian software engineers are working as low-cost consultants to a variety of American computer firms; the venerable—and last remaining—American motorcycle manufacturer, Harley-Davidson, is having all the design and prototype work on its newest motorcycle engine done in Germany by Porsche, A.G. At the moment it is not a lack of technical excellence that drives these American companies overseas; it is cost. But as more firms go offshore for their services, the domestic service industries will suffer and will lose their state-of-the-art status.

Today much of the service and information sector is already dominated by foreign firms—the five largest banks in the world are all Japanese, as is the top insurance firm. The Japanese also have the world's largest advertising agency—Dentsu—and their trading companies dominate many of the sensitive import/export markets. Foreign firms are also coming into the United States in a big way, buying up our companies or establishing companies of their own. The Japanese financial giant Nomura Securities has moved onto Wall Street and almost overnight become a major underwriter of new stock issues; Mitsui, the big, diversified Japanese banking and trading house, now owns a string of U.S. banks; the British now own three of our five largest advertising agencies, and Saatchi and Saatchi, the biggest British advertising conglomerate, is rapidly acquiring not only our advertising firms but also our marketing and consulting firms, making it one of the world's largest "information" companies almost overnight. The list of foreign acquisitions is growing too fast to keep up with and with each acquisition we lose a certain measure of control over our own economy.

There is another problem with the service and information sector that observers like Naisbitt and other futurists have failed to see. Except for very key, even strategic, elements within this sector, the bulk of the jobs simply represent added levels of bureaucracy, red tape, and overhead. Large numbers of these jobs will ultimately be automated, jobs now performed by salespeople, bank tellers, and typists, for example, curtailing their value as means for generating employment. But for each productive worker (someone, that is, who collaborates on making something) there are dozens of people who must be supported, often at great expense. Managers, inspectors, government workers, insurance agents, bankers, lawyers (surely a profession that thrives on obstructing productive enterprise), market researchers, travel agents, and others in this vein really produce nothing on their own; they merely moderate the activities of the more productive sectors. Even so, we continue to produce many times more service sector workers than we do productive workers. For example, there are currently ten times more business majors than physical science majors and three times as many business majors as engineering majors in our universities and colleges. Whether or not a service economy is desirable, we are certainly producing an abundance of workers for it.

Our problem is not just the shift in emphasis from production of goods to production of services, but the growing lack of competitiveness of the economy as a whole. Today we are losing our manufacturing sector in which are invested trillions of dollars—not to mention the lives of millions of workers. Good-news gurus may say that the loss of these basic industries is good and that it marks an inevitable transition from one age to the next, but just why it is inevitable and whether it is good must certainly be ascertained. At the same time, we must also ask ourselves whether the change from a high-wage production economy to a low-wage service economy is desirable. We must ask this especially since even low-wage services are also subject to intense competition—competition we may lose. The transition that Naisbitt and others foresee is far too dangerous to leave to the workings of the "invisible hand" since our national and personal wealth is at stake.

More important, futurists like Naisbitt fail to put the growth of the information economy into proper perspective. As a nation we must be able to compete with other countries—as the Japanese do so successfully—by adding more intellectual content to our products and to the factories that produce them. If we focus the attention of our best designers and engineers on the task of manufacturing world-class products, then we can keep our high-wage workers busy making goods that are competitive with those made anywhere. But we have not been devoting enough intellectual energy to innovation; as a result, manufacturing has suffered and wages have shrunk.

Without a doubt manufacturing is becoming more complex

and product design increasingly demanding. Because the tasks at hand are more demanding does not mean that we can simply walk away from manufacturing—the prime generator of wealth in our land—and say that it no longer matters. To justify our retreat from production by saying we will provide only services can only accelerate the downward path we have been treading for more than a decade. While we may produce more information than any other nation, information produced for its own sake has little value. What is crucial is the application of knowledge to create wealth and to improve our lives, and that comes from increasing the intellectual content of our products and processes. If we continue shifting manufacturing jobs overseas, soon the information and service sector jobs will follow. And then what will happen to America? What will we do to support the lifestyles we have learned to enjoy but can now scarcely afford?

3

TUMBLING FROM THE HEIGHTS OF POWER

DURING the presidency of Harry S. Truman, that pugnacious little man from Missouri with perhaps the greatest knowledge and understanding of history of all our modern presidents, the United States was an awesome power. We were the only major country to have emerged from World War II with our factories, farms, roadways, and ports unscathed, enabling us to resume our peacetime production without skipping a beat. During Truman's second term, in 1950, the United States produced over 40 percent of the world's goods and services and held more than 70 percent of the world's gold reserves. In 1950, with a population considerably under 200 million people, our engines of industry generated nearly half the world's wealth while the economies of Europe and Japan lay in ruins. Stuttgart, Frankfurt, Nuremberg, Berlin, Cologne, Munich, Dresden, Tokyo, Hiroshima, Nagasaki—all were reduced to twisted heaps of wreckage while our cities remained untouched.

Not only did we dominate the world economy in 1950,

we also dominated its institutions and imagination as well. Hollywood turned out a steady stream of movies that were seen by countless millions around the world. James Dean, Marlon Brando, Marilyn Monroe, Jerry Lewis, Gregory Peck—the list is long—were as familiar to audiences in France, Spain, Britain, Japan, and Mexico as any of their own stars. The music of Elvis Presley, Nat King Cole, Jerry Lee Lewis, and a host of others permeated the airwaves even behind the iron curtain, teaching American values and amplifying American social conflicts. The Soviet Union spent millions of rubles on propaganda but the biggest advertisements for America and our free and democratic way of life came from the creative outpouring of our media and from the flood of sturdy, well-engineered, and well-constructed American products streaming from our factories in seemingly limitless supply. Mack trucks, Evenrude outboards, Dodge pickups, DCs, Cessnas, and Pipercubs, IBM typewriters, Chris Craft boats, Ampex tape recorders became well-built fixtures seen in almost every country of the world.

During Truman's term the American beat was the rhythm that moved the world, not just in the field of entertainment, but in politics and economics as well. As Truman's representative, Eleanor Roosevelt served as our chief delegate to the fledgling United Nations, defining that organization's humanitarian objectives and leading what was then a staunchly pro-American majority. Under Truman's direction, the World Bank was established to help reconstruct Europe and the International Monetary Fund was created to make short-term loans to help keep world trade growing.

Truman took other bold initiatives as well. After the war, Greece, which had been invaded and then brutally occupied by the Nazis, was beset with a guerrilla insurgency backed by the Soviet Union. With Britain too weak and the rest of Europe still in shambles, Truman sent Dwight Griswald and a contingent of marines to Greece to put a swift end to the guerrilla war. In the process of driving out the Communists and restoring democracy to the country that gave birth to that idea, Truman established the NATO alliance of Western

European countries and the United States to contain the post-war expansion plans of the Soviet Union. Shortly after, he established similar pacts in parts of Asia, the Middle East, and Latin America and decided to stand firm by committing troops to Korea under the United Nations flag. In the seven hectic years of Truman's presidency, an entirely new international system was established based not on colonial power but on national sovereignty, a host of interrelated and more or less democratic international institutions, such as the United Nations and the World Bank, and growing international trade. In this postwar system, which scholars have called the "second try at world order" (after colonialism's first attempt), the United States assumed the leadership role not because it was a "neocolonialist" power controlling the destinies of smaller countries through covert means (although this was one of the old elements in the new system), but because the United States' weight in the world economy was so considerable it alone could guarantee the integrity of the trading system and support the military forces necessary to contain the Soviet Union.

How well did the world economy work when we were managing it properly? America loaned European governments the money to rebuild their devastated cities under the Marshall Plan, we shipped food to Europe by the boatload, and in some cases even airlifted supplies overseas. Our technicians, engineers, and machines were sent overseas to help rebuild factories and to establish new rail lines and roadways, and we trained a generation of foreign students at our colleges and universities. We sent coal from Virginia to warm the inhabitants of Europe during the cold winters after the war and we shipped oil from Texas to restart the engines of production. No other nation but the United States was strong enough to rebuild the war-ravaged continent of Europe and the country of Japan, and when that task was finished, under cost and ahead of schedule, we set our sights on building up the third world.

During the period of the 1940s through the late 1960s world trade grew at unprecedented levels. Our dollar-based world trading system was productive enough to enable world output to more than double in the first fifteen years after the war. From 1948 through 1971 trade expanded at an incredible 7.27 percent per year, raising hundreds of millions of people, in different societies worldwide, from abject poverty to a middle-class life-style in little more than a generation. Had this dazzling economic performance continued through the seventies and into the eighties, and had it not been accompanied by dramatic increases in population, the world of today would be considerably different, with poverty perhaps eradicated from the planet and the American engine of global growth pulling the world to ever higher levels of wealth.

The train analogy for America's role in the world economy is an apt one. In the postwar system the United States was conceived of as the world's technological leader, with a large number of highly paid sophisticated workers producing expensive, high-tech products for the rest of the world. Our exports of high-tech products were supposed to guarantee that our workers would be the most productive and the best paid, giving them the buying power necessary to purchase the exports of less sophisticated countries. In practice, we would build the world's jumbo jets, which would give our workers the wages to buy large volumes of low-tech imports of textiles, shoes, and raw materials from abroad. Heavy investment in our forefront technologies would keep us at least a few dozen steps ahead of the other rapidly developing countries, like Japan and Germany, and assure our role as the "leader of the pack," while our major universities and government research centers would work hard to maintain and further our technological lead.

This postwar system was probably the closest we have ever come to devising a national plan for economic growth—and it worked splendidly. Clark Kerr, the chancellor of the University of California during the late 1950s and early 1960s, saw his sprawling campuses and research complexes as part of a national effort to keep our nation at the leading edge of technology and our economy far in front of any competition by training as many students as possible in the sciences. And until Governor Ronald Reagan took office in California, replaced Clark Kerr, and began cutting the university budget, Kerr's vision of the university as one of the most important elements in maintaining our nation's competitiveness remained intact.

President John Kennedy shared the idea that America's economy could only fulfill its global function if it remained at the leading edge of science and technology. As president, Kennedy provided generous funding to our various national institutes of science and technology, like the National Institutes of Health, National Institute of Science, and National Aeronautics and Space Administration, which would in turn either carry out their own research or fund university and independent research centers to extend the limits of our knowledge. He also committed billions of dollars to putting a man on the moon within the decade with full cognizance of the commercial spinoffs that would accrue from this highly specialized research and technological effort. In this way, industry could benefit from its own research and from research that might be too costly for the private sector to undertake or that might not have any commercial application in the short term. And industry could also commercialize developments made during the large-scale pioneering programs like the race to the moon.

But to retain our leadership position in the world economy and to support our high-wage, high-consumption society, we had to remain ahead of other countries in the most vital research areas simply because modern industry is knowledge driven. In the early 1960s, when the Russians launched the world's first artificial satellite, Sputnik, we could say their lead in space research was an accident, redouble our efforts, and overtake them in the race to put a man on the moon. In the 1960s we were rich, our national income was rising, we could afford to commit the large sums of money needed to say ahead; and perhaps most important, there was the political will to back these large-scale efforts.

But since the early and mid-1970s we have lost vital ground in a number of very important areas with dramatic economic consequences for our future; and today we have less money available, and less political will, to enable us to catch up with the leaders. For instance, with the Challenger space shuttle disaster, we have once again lost our leadership role in space research to the Russians, who have recently tested a new generation of heavy-lift booster rockets and their own advanced reusable shuttle. They have also begun launching satellites for other countries at commercial rates, and now maintain a permanent human presence in space, as well as a permanent, orbiting space station.

We have been leapfrogged by the Japanese in advanced-generation chip and computer design (the so-called fifth generation), in the production of new ceramics for automobile and aircraft engines, in the areas of fermentation and enzyme technology, cheap chemicals, and even plastics, and in a number of vital areas of metallurgy for making jet engines and high-temperature alloys. The Japanese have also surpassed us in the vital area of process engineering, which is the bedrock of manufacturing, and in robot technology—all very vital areas for the future. In other words, our technological lead has been eroded and seriously undermined.

While everyone looked nervously to the Japanese, the Chinese overtook us in superconductor research, with far-reaching implications for everything having to do with electricity, from power transmission to making supermagnets and supermotors. Superconducting technology is expected to be a vital area for the future that will have impact on nearly every aspect of tomorrow's economy.

And while we have been complacent about our lead in commercial aviation, the Europeans have started producing wide-body airplanes many critics say are superior to our own.

I have composed this very short list to illustrate in what areas of science and technology we have lost our lead. It is not exhaustive by any means, but simply points out that our lead has vanished precisely in those areas that will be of primary economic importance in the years to come. Without regaining momentum with respect to new materials, superconductors, computer design, space and aircraft construction, and manufacturing and process technology, there is no way that our work force can be anything more than low-wage workers supplying the Europeans and Japanese with raw materials in exchange for their high-tech products. By losing vital ground in these areas American workers will, by necessity, fall farther down the wage scale, and the quality of our lives will diminish even more.

In world terms, this fall from leadership is nothing new. Until the eve of World War I, Great Britain was the world's wealthiest nation and the most advanced technologically as well. During the heyday of the empire, British scientists and engineers led the world in the development of steam power, shipbuilding, manufacturing technology, biology, electricity, and in many other areas. Even in the period immediately before World War II, British scientists were still capable of occasionally dazzling the world with their insights—they invented radar and the jet engine and discovered penicillin. Yet, with the loss of scientific and technological leadership they also lost their economic leadership. In a manner very much prefiguring our own decline, the British began to slide down the wage ladder just after World War I in their own Decline and Crash. They have gone from the premier world power with the globe's best-paid workers to one of Europe's poorest nations overtaken in standard of living and in wage rates not only by Germany, France, Switzerland, the Netherlands, and the Nordic countries, but now by Italy as well. And while there are many differences between the United States and Britain, one character flaw we both share is an abhorrence for developing a national economic plan. It was the British, after all, who developed the idea of the "invisible hand."

To keep the United States at the center of the world system and to keep the world system functioning smoothly require not only that we maintain our lead in the high-tech sector but also that world trade expand in an orderly way. But for the last seven years global trade either has remained flat or has been contracting and, as a result, has been robbing the world of its wealth and the citizens of the world of their individual gains. A world economy that has only spotty, unequal growth, with pockets of economic contraction, translates into world of political uncertainty and upset. A globe in which trade is stagnant or contracting also translates directly into the loss of markets for American exports. In this condition of stagnant world trade, the country most adversely affected has been the United States—not Japan, Germany, or South Korea—because it is our traditional overseas markets that have dried up, only to compound our woes. But more will be said about this later.

Even though we are losing our lead as the world's largest high-tech exporter, we have maintained our position as the world's largest importer of goods, which has created our huge trade deficits. Because we have ceased to offset our huge imports with equal or greater exports we have perverted the functioning of the world system. Today, because we import so much more than we export and spend so much more than we earn, the United States is no longer a net creator of wealth but a net generator of debt. With flagging innovation, lackluster spending on science and technology outside of the Defense Department, and with few goods to export, we are financing our imports by borrowing money from domestic sources and from abroad. What's even worse, though, is that since the dollars we pay to foreigners for their products do not return to our shores to be used in payment for our products, we are flooding the world system with U.S. money that stays abroad, weakening not only our own economy but also the entire world economy.

The gigantic exodus of dollars from our shores is not a new phenomenon. We have been weakening our economy and the world system for at least twenty-five years. Small deficits began to show up even in the 1960s, resulting from the costs of military and developmental foreign aid, the expense of maintaining American soldiers and their families overseas at nearly five thousand large and small bases, and the heavy foreign investments made by our multinational corporations that, even then, were eager to find cheaper places to manufacture their products. During the 1960s, Ford bought a large share of Mazda Motors and GM bought into Isuzu while Levi Strauss, ITT, IBM, and Singer sewing machines, to name just a few, opened factories around the world, all with long-term consequences for our domestic workers and all cutting into our exports. And when the Vietnam War moved into full swing the exodus of dollars grew even larger.

President Kennedy ranked our emerging balance-of-payments problems just under thermonuclear war in terms of its potential to harm the country. Because we were moving our manufacturing plants offshore, importing more, and exporting less, the pool of dollars held overseas (primarily in Europe, where they became known as Eurodollars) grew wildly. By the end of the 1960s it is estimated that there were as many as 100 billion Eurodollars held in banks and used for financial transactions around the world. By the mid-1970s there were about 500 billion to 700 billion Eurodollars, and now there are as many as 1 trillion Eurodollars, or even more, that never will be "repatriated" to buy our domestically made products.

From the standpoint of our economy, the consequence of having so many dollars floating freely around the world is devastating. This money can be deposited in banks, loaned and reloaned, all the while creating even more money as it tumbles through the international banking system. For instance, if you deposit 100 Eurodollars in a bank in Paris, I can go to that same bank, borrow that $100, and deposit it in another bank where it can be loaned out again, this time to someone else. As a result of this type of transaction, your original $100 deposit has mushroomed into $300— your $100 credited to your account, the $100 I borrowed from your bank, and the final $100 loaned to someone else. This type of money creation, subject to just the barest rules and regulations, can go on and on. Yet, even though this money creation occurs beyond our shores and outside of our banking rules, the U.S. government is still responsible for making sure that they retain their value. This means that when it comes to setting the rates of exchange for the dollar it is not sufficient simply to think only in terms of the value of our home-grown currency. We must also consider how to keep 1 trillion in overseas dollars from exerting an undesired effect on our exchange rates.

In the late 1960s, however, when there were "only" 100 billion or so Eurodollars in existence, our Treasury Department was obligated to convert those dollars into gold at the offical rate of $35 per ounce. This was the cornerstone of the postwar system—a stable and freely convertible dollar for use in world trade. The only trouble was that there was only about $14 billion worth of gold in Fort Knox to cover 100 billion Eurodollars, as well as the billions of dollars at home.

This large and growing discrepancy between the number of paper dollars in the world and the amount of gold in Fort Knox made many people nervous, but none more so than General Charles de Gaulle, the president of France from early 1956 until 1968. De Gaulle fancied himself and France as the two most important of God's creations, although he often thought of himself as the personification of France, thereby reducing God's important creations to just one.

De Gaulle also detested Kennedy for his youth, wealth, and what he regarded as his bias toward Britain in the guise of the famous "special relationship" under whose terms we shared our atom bomb secrets with the English but not with the French. To punish Britain, not just for its close friendship with the United States, but also for the way Churchill disdained him during World War II, de Gaulle tried with a good deal of success to keep Britain out of the newly emerging European Common Market.

Most of all de Gaulle was intensely suspicious of America's ability to lead the world and protect the stability of the international economy. This was of paramount importance because de Gaulle remembered only too well how the depression of the 1930s had plunged the world into war and had led to France's occupation by the Nazis and to its international humiliation. In de Gaulle's modest opinion, the only nation capable of leading the postwar world was France; America was too immature, too untrustworthy, and too much of an international upstart. While France had managed an empire for more than two centuries, America was not yet even two centuries old.

But de Gaulle was also a practical man, a shrewd politician, and a keen and difficult negotiator. He did not want France to be last in line when it came to converting his nation's growing holdings of dollars into gold at the official rate. He understood very clearly that if there were a panic run to convert the 100 billion or so of Eurodollars into gold, very soon the U.S. Treasury Department, because of its meager resources, would have to suspend its obligation to convert those dollars into gold. If this were to happen, the value of the dollar would plummet and the world system might collapse. He also knew that if there were a run on the dollar, and its value could not be supported, then the price of gold would soar, since it would be the only safe investment. De Gaulle therefore wanted all French Eurodollars converted into gold to protect his nation's economy in the event of America's inability to back the dollar with gold.

From our vantage point it is very difficult to grasp the significance of the rapid buildup of Eurodollars and de Gaulle's attempts during the 1960s to convert France's pool of dollars into gold, particularly because the direct gold-to-dollar link was severed by the stroke of a pen in 1971. But de Gaulle's attempt to convert his country's considerable dollar holdings into gold was in fact a frontal attack upon the postwar system itself and the first direct challenge by an "ally" to America's postwar leadership, and it culminated in his final attempt to bring down the dollar in 1968. Despite pleadings from then-president Lyndon Johnson and the urgings of the other European leaders not to attempt to destroy the postwar system, de Gaulle insisted on pressing for convertibility.

Both countries were measurably weaker when de Gaulle abandoned his assault on the dollar, in 1968. France's dollar holdings were virtually depleted while our gold stocks had dwindled to less than half of what they had been in 1950.

While it is fortunate that the French government alone did not have the dollars to empty Fort Knox, ill will was in the air to the extent that de Gaulle even pulled France out of the military arm of NATO—another United States-led international institution. We had survived this first attack upon our economic leadership, but only barely. And what's more, even with the memory of de Gaulle's raid on the dollar fresh in our minds, we still made no real effort to ensure the future strength of the economy.

While it is true that during de Gaulle's assault on the dollar President Johnson did enact a number of half-hearted rules to stop the further erosion of the American economy, it was a case of too little too late. These measures recognized the growing problems confronting the American economy and tried to address them by stimulating exports, limiting the flow of dollars overseas, limiting foreign investment, enhancing our relationships with the third world, and stabilizing the value of the dollar, but in practice Johnson's rules and regulations were in effect for too short a time, less than a year, and with too few teeth to strengthen the economy to any degree. Johnson's measures prohibited all American multinational companies from investing in continental Europe while limiting investment in Britain, Australia, Canada, and Japan (four countries that had aided us against de Gaulle) to 65 percent of their 1965–1966 levels. U.S. exports were to be promoted through special loan programs especially aimed at the third world, American tourists traveling abroad were subject to limitations on the amount of dollars they could convert into other currencies, and American banks were subject to lending restrictions abroad while military recruits lost some of their benefits for serving overseas.

Johnson attempted to restrict the outflow of dollars with these measures, but he accelerated their exodus, and our decline, by increasing our involvement in the Vietnam War. With as many as 550,000 troops committed to Vietnam, and our ships and planes crossing the Pacific constantly to give them the necessary support, the stream of dollars leaving our shores grew rapidly. During the entire Vietnam era, other overseas defense programs were allowed to continue without restraint, spewing dollars out into the world like blood from so many wounds.

Not only did the steady flow of dollars overseas do us real damage, but because Johnson continued with his other pet projects, the war on poverty and the space program, without raising taxes, the economy was dealt a further blow with the rapid accumulation of inflationary debt. Johnson, who was perhaps too effective a manipulator of Congress, was able to convince our legislators to fund his programs and the war by printing money and issuing bonds instead of raising taxes. These newly created dollars and the debts that went with them pressed against the postwar system severely. Even an economy as rich as ours was in the 1960s could not afford to fight wars and defeat poverty without raising taxes. The combined effect of the accumulation of federal debt and the exodus of dollars overseas was too great. In the end, as an exhausted Lyndon Johnson made his exit from public life, it was already becoming apparent that not only were we losing the war in Vietnam and the war on poverty, but we were destroying our own economy as well.

As a result of de Gaulle's attack on our Treasury, the Vietnam War, the war on poverty, and the years of neglecting exports and domestic manufacturing, the U.S. dollar of today is a very different creature from the U.S. dollar that existed from 1945 to 1971. Unlike the dollar of the past, today's greenback has a wildly fluctuating value against other currencies and no official link to gold. With its value fixed at $35 per ounce of gold, the dollar of the past represented something substantial and absolute. It was a yardstick against which other currencies could be measured. Unless a nation was experiencing a catastrophe, its money kept its value based upon a fixed and established conversion rate into dollars. For years there were five French francs to the dollar, three German marks to the dollar, and the British pound was worth a little more than two dollars. But today, the dollar fluctuates wildly. From 1945 to 1971, as already mentioned, an ounce of gold was by law worth exactly $35, but in 1978, seven years after having been set free from its link to gold, an ounce of the yellow metal cost more than $800. In 1982 gold fell to $300 per ounce, while in 1987 after the market crash that same ounce of gold climbed above the $460 level. What does this represent? No change in the way gold is used in the world, but tremendous changes in the value of the dollar not just against gold but against other currencies as well.

Just think what the ups and downs of the dollar mean to exporters of machine tools and robots. For Cincinnati Milicron, our premier robot maker, exports have been fluctuating greatly. A robot offered for sale might be priced at $30,000, but for a French importer of that product the cost would vary considerably depending on when the product was delivered. If, for example, the robot arrived in France in April 1985 it would cost about 270,000 French francs, using the exchange rate of the day. If, on the other hand, it arrived in France in November 1987 it would cost only 153,000 French francs, because during the interm the dollar dropped in value against the franc. In June 1987 the French importer might be very tempted to buy the Cincinnati Milicron product, but what if the dollar has recovered in value when he must buy spare parts or a second system to complement the first? He has no way to forecast his future costs. If, however, a Japanese multinational like Fujitsu offers a similar product priced in the better managed, more stable Japanese currency, the French importer will have a good idea of his future replacement costs and will be able to make more accurate forecasts. The same is true for other products imported by other countries around the world. When the dollar shifts, uncertainty reigns and trade is threatened.

But the volatile dollar works a two-way street. Suppose a French wine exporter wants to sell his product in New York. In April 1985 he could sell as much Bordeaux as he wanted at 35 francs per bottle because New York wholesalers paying in dollars were able to get the wine for only $3.50 per bottle. But by November 1987, with the dollar falling rapidly, that same bottle cost almost $7. Add shipping, tax, and typical retail markups and the bottle of Bordeaux then sells for about $17 in the liquor store, competing unfavorably against California wines priced far lower. Yet, even at $17 per bottle, the French exporter makes no more money on the deal since his costs and expenses are both figured in French francs.

For exporter and importer alike, the bouncing dollar makes long-term commitments difficult. In the minds of the foreign importers of U.S. products, whether jumbo jets or California oranges, tomorrow's prices are anybody's guess and they will have a powerful incentive to seek more predictable sources, such as the Germans and the Japanese, who carefully limit any fluctuations in their currencies.

Companies that export to the United States also find the American market difficult to forecast, which means that the United States' roles in the postwar system as the world's major market for goods and services, as the primary high-tech exporter, and as the guarantor of the international medium of trade, the dollar, have all been seriously undermined, placing our nation and the world system in general in a very difficult economic position. Add to this our serious and progressive shift down the wage ladder and the prognosis for the future is not good. Any boss in any normal corporation whose management resembled our management of the far more important international economy would soon be told by his company's board of directors, "You can be replaced."

VOLATILE exchange rates increasingly force all partners to look to the short term—exactly what Truman, Eisenhower, and Kennedy wanted to avoid in building up the postwar world economic system. In fact, it was Kennedy's dream to have a world trading system not only free of large-scale currency shifts, but also relatively free of tariffs and other barriers to trade. Talks on seriously reducing trade tariffs were even named the "Kennedy Round" of discussions, in his honor.

Although the dollar of today bears little resemblance to its post–World War II, pre-1971 namesake, it still must carry on its function as the only truly international trading currency. This was the role that was envisioned for the "good-as-gold" dollar in the Bretton Woods Agreement of 1944 as written by the American under secretary of the treasury, Harry Dexter White, and the pioneering British economist John Maynard Keynes.

But with the dollar's nature changing, as the expediency of the moment replaced longer term interests, much of the Bretton Woods Agreement had to be scrapped. Richard Nixon, not exactly famous for his candor, told the world that "we are all Keynesians now," while simultaneously destroying the cornerstone of Lord Keynes's Bretton Woods international economic system.

In 1971, when Nixon dissolved the dollar-to-gold link, he transformed the one global currency the world had from a form of equity, with its value directly linked to a quantity of gold, to a form of debt. It was a reverse alchemy whereby something of extraordinary value, the dollar, became just another form of debt—the federal government's promise to pay each dollar holder not gold or silver, but, incredible as it may sound, simply other dollars. And how much would these dollars be worth now that they were "backed" by the word of the government instead of by gold? It all depended on the day, the market, and which country was interested in trading its currency for our own and buying our products.

Where once the might of our industrial technologies and the quality of our goods created an almost unquenchable thirst for our exports and supported the value of the dollar (people must buy dollars to pay for our products), now the situation is reversed. Only by fiddling with the value of the dollar can America push its exports abroad. With Nixon having made such a tremendous and unsettling change in the world system without consulting any of our allies, it is no wonder that when Reagan asked then Japanese prime minister Yasuhiro Nakasone and West German chancellor Helmut Kohl for help with our exports at Venice he received polite nods of assurance but no real action.

To change the value of the dollar, in the first of several

failed attempts to boost our exports, Treasury Secretary James Baker called together an international group of governmental central bankers for a meeting in September 1986 at the Plaza Hotel in New York. There, behind closed doors and in elegant surroundings, Baker told the assembled guests that he thought the value of the dollar was too high, and he outlined what the exchange rates between the dollar and other currencies ought to be. There was probably a great deal of haggling during those closed-door sessions and a great deal of debate, but within a very few months governments everywhere were selling off their dollars to flood the international currency markets with them. This depressed the dollar's price until it lost more than 40 percent of its value against the German mark, Japanese yen, French franc, Dutch guilder, and so on—not because of any change in demand for our currency or our products, but to use political pressure to compensate for a decade and a half of poor business practices and bad economic decisions. By the following year the dollar lost even more ground.

Paper currencies were not intended to be used politically or to boost temporarily the exports of one or another political constituency—there are other instruments for doing that. The postwar dollar was linked to gold precisely to guard against that kind of manipulation. International currencies, like the dollar of today and the British pound before it, were created as "stores of value," as any first-year economics text explains, to ensure predictability, stability, and a set value during turbulent as well as prosperous times, and to dampen the wild swings in prices that sometimes occur. Like the original meter bar used for measuring distances and kept in a Paris vault, currencies traditionally have also been used as an agreed-upon measure of something of standard value—a commodity like an ounce of gold or silver, for instance. When currencies must be devalued to lubricate the economy—whether in ancient Rome, colonial Spain, or postwar Great Britain—the problem lies not with the currency but with the inability of a nation to create real wealth and to produce products efficiently for the world market.

The necessity of devaluing the dollar by more than 40 percent against some currencies means that, prior to that action, many of our products were not competitive at all. But even with this 40 percent drop in the price of American goods overseas, exports have hardly picked up. That such a drop has not boosted exports is disheartening enough, but it is scandalous that no one in the Reagan administration seemed to be watching as trade gap went from positive, when Reagan was elected, to more than $140 billion in the red by 1986.

THE CONSEQUENCES of severing the link between the dollar and gold have been multifaceted. We were the short-term gainer, but in the long term we are the loser. We gained in the short term because many foreigners took their unbacked dollars and used them to buy U.S. Treasury securities—our primary governmental debt instrument. In effect, they had no other choice but to buy these debt instruments because if they had sold all their dollars to buy other currencies, the dollar's value would have collapsed irretrievably, plunging the world into financial chaos. Treasury securities, issued to raise money to finance our national debt, became the preferred resting place for foreign dollars.

Economic historian and author Michael Hudson, a balance-of-payments expert at Chase Manhattan Bank during the early 1970s, confirms this notion. He explained at a meeting at the United Nations, that the move to buy Treasury notes with overseas dollars was "a well-conceived plan to force foreigners to loan dollars back to the U.S. Treasury to cover our years of deficit spending. In effect, these foreign dollar holders had no choice but to loan their money back to us or see the value of their holdings wiped out. Our debt had been substituted for a real asset."

In all fairness to Nixon, when he cut the link between the dollar and gold, he also tried to strengthen the economy as a whole but his economic package was not sufficient. Along with suspending the convertibility of dollars into gold at the old offical rate, Nixon also enacted comprehensive wage and price controls, slapped a 10 percent surcharge on imports, cut government spending, raised taxes, and agreed with our major trading partners to devalue the dollar to a maximum of 17 percent against other currencies to boost exports. But exports did not recover sufficiently. The import surtax was lifted and the Vietnam War continued and with it a flood of dollars leaving for foreign shores. Like his predecessor, Lyndon Johnson, Richard Nixon recognized the economic problem confronting our nation but was unable, or unwilling, to tackle it completely.

The long-term loss is the unpredictability of the world economy and the major shift from productive investments in new plants and processes, with long-term payback periods, to short-term, more speculative investments in nonproductive assets, such as gold, silver, commodities, and real estate, which have been bought, traded, and developed far beyond real need. In fact, during the early 1970s, the prices of nearly all tangible assets and commodities rose to record or near-record levels as the dollar began to float and fall. The price of art, from the Old Masters to the work of the Tibetan masters, soared, as did the prices of diamonds, emeralds, and other precious stones. In 1967 a one-karat investment-grade diamond cost less than $1,000, but by 1973 its value had climbed to $10,000 and by 1979 to $50,000 before falling back below $10,000 in the early 1980s.

Diamonds, emeralds, and the paintings of the Old Masters can be considered luxuries, but necessities were equally affected. Between 1967 and 1973, lumber prices jumped 82 percent; farm commodities rose by 60 percent; fuel and power supply prices climbed by 31 percent (and this was before the large OPEC price hikes); and metal prices rose by 30 percent.

Commodity prices were going wild, as the dollar lost its tether, but demand, especially during the 1970s, increased only moderately. Speculators rushed into the market while cartels exercised control over supplies to push up prices even further. During the 1970s everything tangible was subject to unstable price inflation. As a result, more money could be made from speculation than from production and there was a shift in America, but not in Japan and Germany and a few other countries that controlled their currencies and inflation, from productive investment to the buying and selling of commodities and other hard assets on a scale not seen since the 1920s.

Rising commodity prices also brought on a new sense of self-confidence (some say arrogance) among the world's commodity-producing countries, many of which were in the third world, and a growing polarization between the rich and poor countries in general. With the stability of worldwide prices ended, the stock market fallen, and the dollar no longer inspiring much confidence, it is no surprise that our political clout in the world also diminished. The shaky dollar also helped bring about the rise of OPEC, and that same dollar is now conspiring with other negative economic events to destroy the value of our assets.

During the 1970s, dollar fluctuations made the long-term investment picture, especially in our own basic industries, like steel, automobiles, and machine tools, too uncertain for financial managers. Plant modernizations and expansions were neglected or delayed and productivity slumped. When the dollar lost its moorings, our physical plants deteriorated and aged so that today we manufacture our products with the industrial world's oldest assemblage of machines (the Dodge main plant in Detroit dates back to 1910). Yet our products must compete with those made by the much newer manufacturing systems of Japan, West Germany, France, the Scandinavian countries, Holland, and Italy, whose industrial leaders were not afraid to invest in their industrial future.

We also lost in the long term because the fall of the dollar caused the price of our real assets to plunge, inviting investors from overseas. In fact, there are now more assets in the United States owned by foreigners than there are foreign assets abroad owned by Americans. Farmland, commercial real estate, and stocks and bonds were bought for a song by overseas investors when the dollar was low. When the rate was $1.70, compared to $1.12, to the pound, British investors bought the A&P chain, Howard Johnson, advertising giant Ted Bates, and then J. Walter Thompson—for years America's largest advertising company. When the yen was at 145 to the dollar, Japanese investors bought a major share of the Shearson Lehman Brothers investment house from American Express, the ARCO Plaza buildings in Los Angeles from Atlantic Richfield, and, before being stopped by the Department of Defense for strategic reasons, tried to snap up the ailing Fairchild semiconductor company. And, when there were only 2 Swiss francs to the dollar, the Swiss bought the Mars candy company and Carnation. Yet, when the dollar was soaring, as late as mid-1986, American companies' foreign acquisitions and investments hardly advanced at all—they were too busy speculating in U.S. commercial real estate.

The fluctuations of the dollar have also cost us thousands of well-paying jobs. In a 1986 study for the Urban Institute, published in the September 1987 issue of *Challenge,* Charles F. Stone and Isabel V. Sawhill showed that there was a relationship between the cost of the dollar and the loss of jobs. For instance, between 1979 and 1984 when the Reagan administration at one point foolishly let the dollar soar to near parity with the British pound, so that millions of Americans traveled to London with empty suitcases to take advantage of the shopping at Harrods, we lost 1.7 million American jobs due to a drop in exports. Which jobs were lost? According to Stone and Sawhill the sector of the economy hardest hit was manufacturing—the bedrock of prosperity and the most expensive and difficult to start anew.

In a 1985 study for the Brooking Institution, Princeton economist William H. Branson found that for every 1 percent appreciation of the dollar there was an additional .4 percent gain in unemployment. Loss of jobs follows rapidly from a soaring dollar, because sales abroad are lost immediately. When the dollar falls it takes far longer to rebuild employment because many companies have gone out of business, have fled the export market altogether, or have been pushed aside at home by stiff foreign competition. We see that now. With the dollar at bargain-basement rates against the yen and mark, exports are barely picking up at all. The balance-of-payments figures have improved with the fall of the dollar, by 1 or 2 percent, only because Americans can no longer afford to import as much as in the past.

IN THE midst of World War II, when the United States was at the height of its power, publisher Henry Luce proclaimed the twentieth century the "American Century." Few could have predicted that the American Century would end after just twenty years. As investment banker Felix Rohatyn recently wrote (*The Twenty Year Century;* New York: Random House, 1983): "From 1965 to date, the American economy has oscillated between growth with inflation and recession combined with unemployment. These oscillations have become steeper as residual rates of inflation and unemployment have increased from one cycle to the next." But just as the swagger and bravado of America is youth faded into a middle-aged bewilderment of uncertain direction and compromised expectations, so has our wealth fallen. The lassitude with which we scrutinized our leaders, presidential as well as congressional, has produced politicians not simply without principles and in debt to their financial backers, but also devoid of vision.

Our lack of a clear-cut public policy to deal with our decline has had a marked effect. Just as in the 1920s, our incomes have fallen and we are kept afloat by constantly increasing levels of debt. Since 1974 the gross national product (GNP) has risen by nearly 260 percent, while debt has risen by almost 300 percent and basic commodity prices have fallen. The average household now carries more than $6,500 in debts, excluding mortgages, and total consumer debt is now equal to about one-fifth of our aftertax income. "We are living in a fool's paradise," Herbert A. Allen, Jr., president of the investment bank Allen & Company, warned in the September 16, 1985, issue of *BusinessWeek:* "I only hope that the dislocations ahead aren't so severe that they cause real suffering."

As First Boston's chief economist, Albert M. Wojnilower told *BusinessWeek:* "If something were to go wrong in the income flows supporting all this debt, the collapse would be worse" than the crash of 1929.

In 1984, corporate debt increased $162 billion over the previous year, while corporate equity plunged nearly $80 billion. Takeover artists rode roughshod over Wall Street using that buildup of debt as fuel for their acquisitions, diverting capital from productive investment. In that same year, 1984, our productivity grew by less than 1 percent. "We've become expert in trading all kinds of financial assets and companies . . . but all the while, productivity still lags," said Paul Volcker, former chairman of the Federal Reserve Board, at Harvard in late 1986, as quoted in the same issue of *BusinessWeek*.

How dangerous are these trends? Professor Kenneth E. Boulding, former president of the American Economic Association, told *BusinessWeek* there is a "positive probability" of another Great Depression. Boulding sees many similarities between 1928 and the days before the October 1987 market plunge:

- The stock market
- The debt situation
- The erosion of profit by interest
- The increasing burden of interest on society
- The unmanageable budget deficit
- The cowardice of Congress as reflected in Gramm-Rudman
- The Pollyanna charm of the president
- The overly successful and rather puzzling control of price inflation
- The big shift which now seems to be taking place in relative prices (in oil, for instance)

Ravi Batra, economic historian, professor, and controversial author, also observed the parallels in *Dun's Business Month:* "Banks earned mediocre incomes during the twenties. They have done much the same in the first half of the eighties. Then, as now, the farm sector was highly depressed because of the loss of foreign markets and the low prices received by American farmers. Then, as now, the coal industry was in the doldrums. So were textiles, shoes, shipping, and the railroads, as they are now. Energy prices declined throughout the twenties. They have done the same so far in the eighties." Batra and Boulding are joined by John Kenneth Galbraith, Charles P. Kindelberger, and scores of other economists who have expressed their deep concern at the similarities between the period just prior to the Great Depression and the present. They also caution against being overly optimistic about our own situation since the October 19 stock collapse by pointing out that it took forty months from the 1929 collapse until the depression hit bottom in March 1933.

Even that normally upbeat cheerleader of capitalism, *Forbes* magazine, sees parallels between the era immediately preceding the Great Depression and now. Ashby Bladen, a financial consultant and author, wrote in the August 25, 1986, issue of *Forbes,* "I no longer think a crash is coming; I think it is here. It has been under way since 1982, but few have recognized it." What are the danger signs Bladen sees? "The Great Depression's main cause was the borrowing spree that financed World War I and then the boom of the twenties. If we had been wise, we would have let it teach us the advisability of restraint with respect to borrowing and spending. Instead, for the last quarter century, we Americans have been off on a borrowing and spending spree that makes our parents look like pikers. . . . [We] have been borrowing heavily abroad, mainly to support a higher standard of living than we are earning by our own productive efforts."

And what collateral is backing such an astonishing increase in our levels of debt? First there is a decade's worth of overbuilt commercial real estate. Then there are the mountains of commodities glutting nearly every world market. Next there is future manufacturing production in a world already reeling from high levels of overcapacity, a condition in which only those industries with the most modern plants will survive. And, finally, there is the word of Uncle Sam.

4

THE DEBT-PROPELLED ECONOMY

ACCORDING to Henry Kaufman, the influential former chief economist of the Wall Street investment firm Salomon Brothers, American debt, governmental, private, and consumer, has jumped from $1.6 trillion in 1970 to $8.2 trillion in mid-1986, as quoted in the September 2, 1986, *Financial Times*. In terms that are on a more human scale, we have gone from debt levels of about $8,000 per person in 1970 to levels that now exceed $40,000 for each American man, woman, and child alive today. And, says Kaufman, our debt is now accumulating far faster than our incomes are growing.

This very disturbing growth in the level of debt is not limited to just the individual and the consumer alone. Every sector of the economy is deeply encumbered in a massive borrowing spree that is choking off our nation's prospects for growth, starving industry of needed investments, and further contributing to the Decline and Crash of the economy.

In previous eras the governmental structure of society strove to limit the growth of debt. Four thousand years ago in the ancient Middle East, the Sumerian civilization, along with the ancient Hebrews and Babylonians, enacted laws requiring that all debts be forgiven every seven or so years. These ancient peoples understood that debt tends to concentrate wealth in the hands of the few as interest rates grow beyond the debtors' abilities to pay. This brings great pain to the society and causes social instability and even the loss of precious ancestral lands through foreclosures. Growing debt, in the ancient world, separated families from their farmlands and created new classes of destitute, landless workers. Because incomes were more or less static in the ancient world any growth in borrowing with interest was accompanied by increased hardships. This was true because interest payments can only be sustained if wealth is increasing and in the ancient world, since wealth remained constant for millennia, creditors were only enriched at the expense of the debtors.

During the Christian Middle Ages and in the ancient Muslim world, the collection of interest was considered a serious crime for the same reason—most incomes were static and could not keep pace with the increased expenditures occasioned by interest payments. Governments eager to prevent the collapse of their societies, and the alienation from the land of the nobility, outlawed any interest charges since, unless incomes grow, interest payments represent serious and detrimental deductions from future earnings. But during the late Middle Ages the payment of interest began to emerge even under the watchful eye of the Church when feudal lords waged war on one another, quickly depleting their treasuries of gold. To get around the Church's injunctions against charging interest, clever money lenders labeled the percentage fees they charged "insurance" and said it was a hedge against loss, not a fee for borrowing funds—a ploy used today in Muslim lands where interest payments are still outlawed. But in the feudal era when dukes and lords were unable to pay their finance charges, they simply arrested their money lenders and accused them of crimes against God and the Church, making money lending a dangerous profession with more than the possibility of financial loss—options not open to us today despite our borrowing frenzy.

When the Industrial Age dawned in England, and with it dramatic and steady increases in average income and overall wealth, society could, for the first time, use debt constructively to finance economic expansion. By borrowing money entrepreneurs could invest in new factories and plants that would generate jobs, produce goods, and bring added levels of buying power to society as a whole. With wages increasing and national wealth growing, the societies of the Industrial Age could safely tolerate debt interest levels far in excess of those considered safe in previous times. The key, however, was, and remains, for debt to grow less rapidly than wages and other income so that repayment comes not as a hardship for future generations but as an ever-decreasing share of tomorrow's earnings. With wealth growing rapidly, debt is wiped out by growth and society can easily repay its obligations, not unlike the way an upwardly mobile family finds it easier to make its mortgage payments as its income rises.

Today, however, wealth is no longer growing more rapidly than debt and the universally feared consequences of debt overtaking wealth creation are beginning to affect us. What are these consequences? Precisely what the ancient Sumerians and Hebrews tried to avoid—growing concentrations of wealth in the hands of a few, the increased polarization between rich and poor with its dreaded potential for social upheaval, and, finally, economic contraction.

The concentration of wealth, which accompanies debt growth in a static or declining society, is now beginning to affect our own country in a way not seen since the years just prior to the 1929 depression. In the 1920s the richest 1 percent of the nation owned more than 36 percent of our country's wealth, more than one dollar out of every three were in the hands of just 1 percent of the country. This dangerous trend has Congress alarmed. Representative David Obey, chairman of the Joint Economic Committee of Congress, recently released a controversial study, completed in 1986, that shows that over the past twenty-five years wealth in the United States has indeed become much more concen-

trated and has been doing so since the mid-1970s—reversing
the trend that began shortly after World War II toward a
more egalitarian distribution of wealth. Facing attacks by
the *Wall Street Journal* and a number of conservative economists, Obey and his researchers stood their ground and proved
that the JEC's figures were, in fact, correct. Wealth in the
United States is indeed concentrating and the top 1 percent
of the economy now control more wealth than at any other
time since the Great Depression. (The top 1 percent now
hold more than 34 percent of our nation's wealth—the same
1929 ratio of one dollar out of every three, up from only
one dollar out of every five of our country's wealth in 1949.)
At the same time, the bottom 5 percent suffer from increased
poverty with more than 32 million Americans, one out of
every seven of us, living below the poverty line. So much
for the magic of the market and the wonders of Reaganomics.

There are many reasons for the increased disparity between
rich and poor in America, including our retreat from high-
wage manufacturing and the deterioration of our schools.
But at least one important element is the enormous growth
in borrowing. Increased borrowing with decreasing incomes
is a recipe for both financial ruin and political disaster. The
ancients, who were able to build durable, long-lived societies
around scarce resources and static income levels, knew this
simple fact well and guarded against its onset. Yet we, in
our comparative youth, have ignored the lessons of the distant
past, and the not so distant Great Depression, by allowing
debt to increase even in an era of negative income growth.

With debt sailing far ahead of wage growth the American
economic pie is truly shrinking for most families. Not only
must most people subsist on less real income, but more of
that income goes into paying back debt. Paying off the interest
on credit cards, auto loans, and home improvement loans
has decreased our buying power and is therefore making
the average consumer less able to keep his fellow workers
employed by buying up the fruits of his neighbors' efforts.

Our federal government, which in normal times should
be acting to protect our society from the evils of debt levels

racing ahead of income growth, is one of the chief offenders since its own spending level far exceeds its income from taxes. Since Ronald Reagan first took office our national debt has more than doubled to pay for a host of scaled-back educational, health, and social programs and the biggest arms buildup since World War II (more has been spent on arms by Reagan during peacetime than was spent during the Korean and Vietnamese wars).

Corporate America is also deeply in hock, and many of our major corporations have been forced to increase their indebtedness toward the limits of sustainability, and beyond, as a result of the recent spate of takeover and anti-takeover moves. The debt profile of a defensive corporate America is beginning to look worrisome, with as much as 40 percent of cash flow in late 1986 going to service existing debt, up from 25 percent in the mid-1970s. In addition, because companies are borrowing like mad to protect themselves, their debt-to-equity ratio climbed toward a jittery 50 percent in mid-1986, which means that half of all corporate assets potentially have claims against them. The current deflationary tendencies that are brewing—with prices in real terms declining in the face of worldwide gluts and oversupply of almost every product and commodity—mean that this monstrous corporate debt will become increasingly difficult to service.

In this Decline and Crash period of debt and decline, the provision of credit and other financial services is now one of the most rapidly growing areas of the economy, but it increases at the expense of our future. A large number of our best companies are moving from retailing and manufacturing into the financial services area because of the greater profits available from lending money rather than making first-class goods. This transition also reflects the fact that, increasingly, accountants and MBAs are taking over from engineers and salesmen to run our companies. While engineers and salesmen know products, MBAs and accountants, with rare exceptions, know only money. Companies like GE, once the leading manufacturer of airplane engines, and which recently abandoned its consumer electronics manufacturing businesses, Avco, and American Can Company, now Primerica and formerly the largest producer of containers, have earmarked financial services as the big growth area for the future. Other companies, like Sears, have also moved from traditional goods-based businesses, such as retailing, into financial services because of the high profit margins associated with money lending since biblical times. Yet, just when many of our companies are in the process of transforming themselves to sell financial services, many of our biggest banks are in trouble for the first time since the Great Depression.

Consumer debt is exploding, and today's wage earners are putting even such mundane, repetitive purchases as groceries on their credit cards since their incomes can no longer support their life-styles. At the same time, new financial "products" like home equity loans have greatly expanded the amount of credit available to the average home owner without requiring any increase in level of income. By using the equity in a home to consolidate or pay off old debts, send a child to college, or, worst of all, pay for the purchase of yet more imported products, the average home owner is, in effect, depleting future wealth and systematically eliminating any ability to endure a prolongued period of economic crisis. While in the past the equity that built up in a person's home through improvements and appreciation was to be preserved at all costs until retirement, today—thanks to our declining incomes and increased debt—home equity is being spent even before it accumulates, which means that at retirement, when Americans traditionally sell their homes to raise enough cash to live out the rest of their lives, they will find that they will be lucky to raise enough cash simply to erase their debts.

Just imagine what the typical home owners of 1950 would think of their profligate progeny of the 1980s. To the 1950s family it would have been unthinkable to borrow against home equity and spend that equity as fast as it accrued, except in an emergency or to raise money to start a new business. The situation faced by many people today is that their homes are gaining in value through appreciation while the size of their assets is actually declining. Increasing the size of our mortgage obligations through home equity loans and second mortgages to support our life-styles would have seemed not only preposterous during the 1950, but downright dangerous for the future. And rightly so.

Before we entered the period of the Decline and Crash, America was educated to believe that debt should be kept at a minimum; it would have been unthinkable to refinance the family home to pay for a vacation cruise or a new car. The majority of Americans during the 1950s still believed that it was better to save for a product and wait than to borrow and buy it today. To our more earnest and frugal 1950s forebears, sobered by their firsthand recollections of the Great Depression, we must appear wickedly wild and reckless as we pile up debt. And for what? To support what increasingly resembles an addiction to consumerism and the purchase of foreign goods. How ironic for a nation with such strong Puritan origins to be teetering on the brink as a result of our foolish tendency to live beyond our means.

The buildup of debt now threatens the very security of the American economy. With so many people leveraged to the hilt, not to mention our debt-plagued federal government and our heavily borrowed corporations, the slightest disruption in the payments process—from a major but otherwise survivable recession, for instance—could today spell deep disaster.

In 1929, years before the growth of installment loans, our nation's reserves of credit were more concentrated in the stock market than they are today, making it far easier to bring down the entire banking system with the collapse in stock prices since, unlike today, speculators could borrow 90 percent of their investment. In those days, the average hard-working American and the average corporation alike put their money in the bank. The banks in turn loaned that money to the big brokerage houses, who then reloaned it to the nation's market speculators to buy stocks.

Borrowed money flooding into the stock market pushed prices skyward, and for those who got out early great fortunes were made. But when the big speculative bubble burst, and prices collapsed, few of the ruined speculators could muster up enough cash to pay back the loans they had used to buy their stocks. With stocks knocked down to but a fraction of their pre-1929 prices, and with no federal bank guarantee system, banks were pressed against the wall. Depositors, panicked by the crash of the market, lined up at banks to retrieve their savings. Not even the strongest banks then (or even today) could survive such a run on their funds by depositors because it takes months, even years in some cases, to call in loans. (Don't forget, to a bank "assets" are not its deposits but its interest-paying loans.) In 1929 these panic runs turned up little cash for the depositors, instead driving nearly four thousand banks out of business. No banking system, even our government-guaranteed system of today, can survive a prolonged panic.

In the 1930s, with no cash on hand, the nation's buying power dried up, factories were shut, workers were fired, and soon even international trade between nations all but ceased. The major international debtor nations of the day, our bankrupt World War I allies, stopped payment on their loans, destroying what was left of the world's banking system and the international economy as well. We were forced to endure a deep, prolonged contraction of the world economy that wiped out nearly sixty years of continuous gains.

Although our debt today is far less concentrated than during the 1920s, it is growing very rapidly and affecting every sector. The financial flows needed to support our escalating level of debt are gargantuan and they contribute to the Decline and Crash by robbing the economy of much-needed buying power and driving up interest rates. With so many people competing for loans, and so little saving, banks and other financial institutions can charge higher premiums and higher interest rates than would otherwise be warranted. Real interest rates, which are measured by subtracting the inflation rate from the interest rate, continue to be high when compared to the 1950s and 1960s and serve as a drag on the economy by making it too expensive for companies to borrow money and invest in modernizing their manufacturing plants. In the 1950s, when the economy was growing rapidly and inflation was nil, real interest rates were about 2 percent, which made it easy for companies to keep their plants modern. Now, during the middle Reagan years, with inflation at about 4 percent and the prime rate somewhere between 9 and 14 percent, real interest rates are between about 5 and 10 percent—too high for companies to make their needed capital investments, but high enough to convince a large number of firms to go into the money-lending business. These high levels of real interest, far higher than the real interest rates in Japan, Germany, and Switzerland (which average only 1, 2, or even zero percent), are important factors in explaining why we have trailed so far behind other advanced countries in raising our rate of productivity and why our standard of living is falling when compared to our competitors overseas.

The reason for our high rates of interest is obvious: The demand for loans in this country is enormous and growing but the pool of available dollars is limited. Demand for loans is growing because the economy is not performing sufficiently to raise the income levels of our workers so they can begin saving again, supply the federal government with needed revenue, or provide companies with cash reserves large enough to protect themselves from being taken over. Starved for income, our citizens must borrow to sustain their life-styles while our equally famished government must also borrow to continue supporting its programs.

The federal government is by far the biggest single borrower, dipping deeply into our domestic capital markets and, when they are depleted and exhausted, diving into the capital markets abroad. Like a vacuum cleaner, the federal government borrows funds that ordinarily would have come to it through taxes had the economy continued to expand as it did during earlier decades.

Each year the federal government borrows hundreds of billions of dollars to keep itself in business. Under Reagan the government has even adopted the schizophrenic policy of increasing spending while, at the same time, cutting taxes.

This is not policy, but a kind of madness. Only a cynical or very short-sighted congressman or senator would approve a plan that raises spending while it lowers taxes, thereby forcing the government to compete for funds in private and international credit markets and driving up interest rates precisely when we need to encourage more investment in industry. And only a president suffering from the same lack of vision would sign such preposterous legislation.

The fact is that since the advent of the Reagan administration the government has been in the hands of men and women who have allowed it to borrow more heavily each year. Just consider the numbers: In 1980, at the end of the Carter administration, government taxes versus spending made for a deficit that equaled about 2.3 percent of our GNP. But in 1986, at the height of the Reagan years and with the government's tax revenue down but its spending up, the deficit more than doubled to a high of 4.8 percent of GNP—a figure almost equal to the nation's defense budget for the same year.

So great is the government's borrowing that it has come to resemble the proverbial pig at the lending trough. These huge borrowings by the government greatly alarmed economists who, a few years ago, coined a new term—"crowding out"—to describe what the federal government does to other borrowers eager to get funds for their business needs. By crowding out other borrowers, economists worried, America would suffer since too few funds would be available, at too high interest rates, for our much-needed (and postponed) industrial rejuvenation.

These worried economists underestimated not only the government's appetite for funds but the eager way in which lenders from overseas would rush in to cater to our desires. Treasury notes and other kinds of bonds issued by our government flooded the world's credit markets and foreign investors grabbed at the opportunity of lending money to the U.S. government. The only problem was that now not only were American economists worried about the crowding-out phenomenon, but European economists also became concerned that our government's appetite for funds would steal needed investment funds from their countries' pools of savings. So far, the federal government's borrowing spree is probably not large enough to crowd out simultaneously investment borrowing in America, Europe, and elsewhere; German, Swiss, and Japanese real interest rates are all still below 5 percent, making investment in those countries still relatively easy. But America's hunger for funds has transformed us for the first time since 1914 into a net debtor country—into the largest debtor country, in fact, with outstanding debts more than double those of Brazil.

In 1987 alone, the government had to borrow $214 billion, a sum equal to the gross earnings of ten corporations the size of IBM, which brought its current outstanding debt over the $2.6 trillion level—about $12,000 for each American. Estimates vary, but if the federal government were to cut down significantly from its more than $12 billion monthly borrowing spree, an amount roughly equal to the combined annual budgets of two cities each the size of New York, then real interest rates would tumble significantly, making it far easier for companies to invest in their futures and lightening the burden on the consumer.

If the federal government balanced its budget, there would be other positive benefits that would be felt by the average person immediately. For example, when the government had a balanced budget, interest rates in the United States hovered at between 3 and 5 percent. With today's variable mortgages, if the government balanced its budget and interest rates plunged from 8 to 10 percent to, say, 4 percent, the average home owner with a thirty-year $100,000 mortgage would save almost $600 per month as his payment fell from about $1,000 to $400 per month. That is equal to a savings of as much as $7,200 per year.

No matter how positive the government has said its tax cuts have been under Reagan, and they have benefited the rich of the country handsomely, they in no way equal the overall gains that would accrue to the country if the federal budget were balanced and the government removed itself from domestic and international credit markets. If, as in the previous example, the average home owner were to suddenly have an extra $7,200 (some of which would no doubt be taxed), just consider how this would stimulate and revive the economy.

If the government balanced its budget interest rates probably would not fall as dramatically as just suggested. But the point is that they would fall, and fall significantly. Most important of all, sharply decreased interest rates would be a much greater boon to prosperity than cutting taxes has been.

Another important consequence of a federally balanced budget would be that the interest rates on foreign loans would also go down. These loans would then be far easier for foreign nations to repay, which would help our banks regain their health and enable the foreign borrowing countries to resume their growth and begin once again to buy our products.

How can the fed stop borrowing? Either cut spending or raise taxes—both very painful, but to different sectors of the population. After all, whose taxes should be raised and whose benefits should be slashed? In the tug-of-war for funds between competing interests the outcome is never completely equitable. In our "no-growth" economy, the military must compete for funds against social welfare programs, which is a little like the competition between a tiger and a goat, with social welfare programs losing out. But there are many ways to increase government revenue constructively (by taxing oil imports, for example) so that the benefits of a freer, low-interest-rate credit market could start the economy growing again.

According to forecasts made by Alan Greenspan and quoted in the August 18, 1986, issue of *BusinessWeek* before he became chairman of the Federal Reserve Board, the average consumer now pays out more than one-third of his income just to service his own personal and growing debt, up from 24 percent in 1983. This figure is for all age groups and it thus camouflages the fact that among younger consumers, who are the most vulnerable to layoffs and firings, the amount spent on debt servicing is far higher than the current 34 percent average. Consumer debt is growing, according to Greenspan, at a rate substantially higher than liquid assets, which only further emphasizes the struggle most families are now having to maintain their life-styles in the face of our national decline. Couple this with the rush to home equity borrowing and we see before us a very troubled, Decline and Crash economy that at any other time would have had our industrial and congressional leaders clamoring for action.

Consider what is happening to our country with respect to borrowing:

1. All types of debts are growing rapidly, driving real interest rates up and choking off new investment.
2. The real value of our assets is declining because we are taking money out of our homes before they have had a chance to appreciate.
3. Our nation's average income, which must ultimately pay for all this debt, is declining.

Clearly, these debt trends are unsustainable and ultimately will lead to further declines in growth, investment, and standard of living.

In the past such a rapid buildup of debt might have had something of a stimulatory effect on the economy. After all, easy access to credit cards enables the average American to spend more, thereby increasing an already considerable buying power. In Keynesian terms, recessions and depressions are cured by such debt-fueled increases in spending. The trouble is, however, that in today's American economy, with so many imported goods flooding our markets, it is not American workers who benefit from debt-led hikes in consumer spending, but those in factories in Asia, Europe, and Latin America. In 1986, which was a good automobile year, Americans imported enough cars to give Nissan, Toyota, and the expensive German car manufacturers record years while at home GM was forced to lay off 29,000 workers. With foreign economies receiving the stimulus from our growth in consumer debt, we are left with larger interest payments that diminish future buying power.

Creating greater consumer debt as a way to encourage increasing economic growth also presents other problems. At a certain point consumers reach their individual credit limits, are forced to cut back on their purchases because of increased interest payments, and the economy loses momentum in a way that is very difficult to regain. This further adds to the downward acceleration of the Decline and Crash.

AS A RESULT of this increase in indebtedness, our financial institutions themselves are in trouble. Just consider what is happening to our banks. L. William Seidman presides over the Federal Deposit Insurance Corporation (FDIC), the federally chartered and funded organization that is charged with guaranteeing against loss the deposits in our commercial banks and in some of our other banking institutions as well. All reports indicate that today Mr. Seidman is worried about the tremendous increases in our levels of debt—34 cents of increase in all types of debt for every dollar increase in income over the last five years—which is a very heavy price to pay for each dollar gain.

With public, corporate, and individual borrowing reaching gigantic proportions and billions in loans to the third world left unpaid, there is growing cause for concern about how our banks can survive. As of late 1986, 1,411 of the nation's 14,000 commercial banks were on Mr. Seidman's FDIC problem list, more than 10 percent of the country's commercial financial system. Outright failures of U.S. banks in 1986 reached a total of 66, while 96 banks had to be shut down in the first half of 1987 alone. Although most of the banks that fail are small and easily merged with larger, more financially sound partners under the FDIC's direction, the banks that are failing are beginning to get larger. Over the last few years we have witnessed the collapse of the Continental

Illinois Bank (now quietly being run by the government); the demise of the giant First Oklahoma Bank & Trust, a major oil bank; the near failure and FDIC-sponsored buyout and guarantee of the First City Bancorporation of Texas, a $12.5 billion institution; and Bank of America's recent announcement of a $640 million quarterly loss and its intention to request a bailout from the Japanese. All of these troubles combined with earlier losses at California's Crocker National Bank and at many of the large Texas banks have put severe strains on the bank guarantee system, especially the FDIC, whose assets total only $10.9 billion. The FDIC's total assets are not even sufficient to bail out one large money-center bank, such as Citibank, Chase Manhattan, Bank of America, Wells Fargo, and others, with individual portfolios in troubled Latin American loans in the billions.

So troubled are the large money-center banks because of their portfolios of bad loans to Latin America that during the first quarter of 1987, they were forced to build up their reserves in a last-ditch effort to protect themselves and their depositors against widespread default by Latin American borrowers. These reserves were enhanced by keeping more cash on hand, instead of loaning it out, and by selling new stocks. Selling new stock makes it harder for dividends to be kept high while curtailing loans hurts income. For the fifteen largest U.S. money-center banks this meant an aggregate operating loss of $10.8 billion for the first quarter of 1987 alone— the largest loss since the Great Depression. And because these banks had to set aside large reserves of funds to cover themselves against those bad Latin American loans, their other reserves, which are set aside as protection against bad domestic and other foreign loans, are stretched dangerously thin, increasing the risk to the nation's banking system.

Part of the problem with the banks' shakiness is due to the underlying weakness of the real economy, rather than of the paper economy of the stock and bond markets. The real economy, that is, the part of the economy that produces wealth, is performing very poorly. Oil prices are down and, short of prolonged war in the Middle East, are not likely to recover significantly; the agricultural sector is in a serious slump with wave after wave of farmland foreclosures; manufacturing, even high-tech Silicon Valley manufacturing, has not come out of the doldrums; new commercial building across most of the nation tapered off; and minerals production is facing a glutted market. These damaged and reeling sectors are also the most heavily in debt. Texas banks, once the shining lights of the banking world, have been pummeled not only by recent drops in oil prices but by decreasing agricultural prices and the slump in Texas real estate as well, factors that have forced even former treasury secretary and Texas governor John Connolly into bankruptcy. With the failure of these sectors of the economy to recover, there will be even more bankruptcies and, with them, more loans that must be written off by already weakened banks.

Slumping commodities prices hurt our banks in two ways. First, the borrower's income declines when the price he sells his commodity for goes down, making him less able to service his debt. This reduction of cash flow is precisely what caused John Connolly and so many others to go bust.

The second factor, of equal importance to banks, is the role that commodities and other real assets play as loan collateral. When a large, troubled Texas bank like Houston's First City made its agricultural, oil, and real estate loans during Houston's boom years of the 1970s and early 1980s, oil cost $38 a barrel, wheat prices were high, and Texas real estate was appreciating wildly. Today, when the cash flow of the borrowers is either down or nonexistent, the value of the collateral to be sold at auction is also down, to a fraction of its value. Farmland in parts of Texas can be had for less than 50 percent of its value in the 1970s, oil prices have fallen 40 percent, and Houston home owners are just walking away from their homes, reducing drastically the value of these assets as collateral. This means that banks are less likely than ever to recover the value of their outstanding loans.

Because a bank's assets are its outstanding loans, not its deposits, a bank is eager to loan out money as quickly as it comes in. A deposit put into a bank means the bank must pay the depositor interest, whereas a loan means the bank is earning money. A depositor's funds are safe only when the bank is prudent in its lending policies, when the economy is healthy enough to sustain wealth, and when the FDIC is there as a final resort. But many argue today that with a shaky economy and so many banks teetering on the edge, the number and value of the "at-risk" deposits across the nation greatly exceed the FDIC's capacities as an insurer. In such a case, the FDIC would have to request emergency funding from Congress, which might in turn force the federal government into even more borrowing or into the inflationary printing of money. In any event, the weakness of the FDIC means that it cannot sustain even a mild "panic" among depositors if they all demand their money from the banks.

Banks are not the only troubled element in our national financial picture owing to the mushrooming of debt. As a group, our nation's savings and loans institutions, the so-called thrifts, are perilously weak. These institutions, which are insured by the FDIC's twin, the Federal Savings and Loan Insurance Corporation (FSLIC), have been experiencing a dramatic increase in their rate of failure and a worrisome flight of funds as nervous depositors put their money elsewhere (from September 1986 to August 1987 more than $25 billion was withdrawn from thrifts by worried depositors). The number and size of thrift failures are now beyond the capacity of the FSLIC and have actually caused this agency to be insolvent from December 1986 through most of 1987. During this period, when the FSLIC was confronted with a deficit of more than $6 billion as a result of bailing out failing thrifts, most of the nation's deposits in these institutions were technically unprotected. This prompted Bill Clements, governor of Texas, to predict that the FSLIC would be able to pay out only 30 cents cash for every dollar on deposit in a thrift, with the remaining 70 cents on the dollar being paid to depositors in the form of ten-year government-backed IOUs. This prediction, which appeared in the August 8, 1987, *New York Times,* was immediately denied by

M. Danny Wall, the chairman of the Federal Home Loan Bank Board, the body that oversees both the FDIC and the FSLIC, but it reflects the level of concern among many of our governmental leaders about the health of our banking and savings and loan system.

So bad has the failure rate been for the nation's thrifts that Wall was forced to appeal to Congress to allow the organization to borrow an additional $10.8 billion in the nation's capital markets to bail out the ailing thrifts and cover existing losses. But the real question is: Why are these savings and loan institutions going broke?

The nation's thrifts are primarily in the mortgage lending business. During the 1950s, 1960s, and early 1970s they prospered mightily by issuing long-term, low-interest mortgages across the country. These organizations get the money they loan out from depositors and from their own borrowing in the commercial credit markets, while their income comes from the loans they make. With so many long-term loans made during the fifties and sixties, when interest charges were only 4 or 5 percent, the thrifts' incomes could not keep pace with the price they had to pay for funds during the high-interest seventies and eighties. On top of that, with the advent of money-market funds with interest rates as high as 18 percent, these institutions lost depositors in droves until they also began to offer high interest rates on deposits. But no institution can long afford to pay out high levels of interest based on an income that is fixed at a much lower level.

This forced the savings and loans into a predicament. They were borrowing in the commercial markets at high interest rates and paying high rates to depositors while much of their income was still pegged to the low-rate mortgage loans they had made decades before. Until the advent of variable-rate mortgages, the thrifts were caught in a terrible cash crunch with their costs of doing business far exceeding their incomes. Furthermore, as the overheated commercial real estate market began to soften in the 1980s, and the rate of mortgage defaults grew, particularly in the South and West, these institutions began to suffer even greater losses, which forced them to go to the FSLIC for help.

The smartest of the thrifts survived the pressures of the late 1970s and 1980s by cutting back drastically, or even stopping, new loans during those periods of soaring interest rates. Others, however, felt that the new, high interest rates gripping the country as a result of the federal government nuzzling at the credit trough were temporary. These thrifts borrowed funds short term from the commercial credit markets while continuing to make long-term loans aggressively. They were hoping for a quick drop in interest rates so that they could then refinance their own borrowing—in much the same way individual home owners do when the rates come down—and return to their old way of doing business. But for these institutions interest rates never fell far enough for them to regain health. And, of course, there were also a number of savings and loans forced into the hands of the FSLIC for such timeless reasons as theft and embezzlement.

In 1986, more than 80 savings and loans received some kind of FSLIC assistance, compared to 57 for the previous year, which was far beyond the FSLIC's guarantee ability and was the prime reason for the $10.8 billion assistance request. This request prompted a proposal from the House of Representatives' Banking Committee for the merger of the FSLIC and the much larger FDIC into one "super" guarantee agency. But many critics protested that the merger of the FDIC and the FSLIC would simply weaken the nation's already troubled deposit guarantee system because so many thrifts would be going under in the next few years. With a spate of closures among the nation's savings and loans, the new "super" agency would have to return to Congress again and again for funds that ultimately the government would have to raise by borrowing (crowding out more productive investment) or by printing money, which is highly inflationary.

Overall, more than $60 billion in bank loans have turned sour, and defaults on corporate bonds topped the $3 billion mark in 1986. The weakness in the credit system and the increase in debt prompted the FDIC's Seidman to worry aloud in a speech to the U.S. League of Savings Institutions at their annual meeting in 1986 that "the great danger is that heavy debt levels will turn a mild or normal business downturn into a severe recession." If we cannot return to a period of growth in real wages, arising from gains in worker productivity, as in the fifties and sixties, then the only way we will be able to underwrite our current levels of consumption will be through a continuous, and unsustainable, growth in borrowing, which will most certainly mean an impoverished future and an acceleration of the Decline and Crash.

During the time President Reagan has been at the helm, piling up monstrous budget and trade deficits, we have been sucked downward, with increasing rapidity, into the vortex of debt. With the sole objective of cutting taxes and raising arms spending, Reagan has succeeded in putting much of our national wealth at risk. And the Tax Reform Act of 1987 has actually taken away many of the tax incentives needed to make further productive investment attractive to business, especially those investments that are required if we are ever to reestablish our industrial leadership. By robbing industry of those needed tax incentives while at the same time competing with private firms for funds in the capital markets, the brains behind the Reagan revolution have set up precisely those conditions that will keep the Decline and Crash on its downward trajectory.

ONE AREA in particular that has dealt a decidedly deadly blow to any attempt at economic recovery is the enormous investment in the military made during the Reagan administration. Military spending represents the single largest increase in the Reagan budgets over the budgets of his predecessors, and as a result is the single biggest reason the government has had to turn to the commercial credit markets.

Although we certainly have a need to defend our nation, and while it is true that the armed forces needed significant upgrading, the consuming military buildup of the Reagan years has damaged the economy. Because the buildup was not funded through an increase in taxation, the price for defending ourselves today will be paid by our children. They will have to foot the bill for the buildup not just with higher taxes but with a decreased standard of living. Just as we are now suffering from a standard of living that has fallen owing largely to Lyndon Johnson's Vietnam War deficit spending, so our children will have to suffer even further declines in their living standards as a result of the Reagan buildup.

The Reagan administration's concentration on military spending has been truly massive: $300 billion was spent in 1986 alone, an amount that analysts remind us is more than enough to wipe out all poverty not only in this country, but in much of the third world as well. Yet this gargantuan sum was spent during an era when our industrial production did not grow.

Even if we disregard such ridiculous expenditures by the military as $7,600 coffee makers, $200 hammers, or $15,000 couches, growth has still been very great in the armaments sector over the last eight years. Unfortunately, this is the least productive segment of the economy since weapons contribute virtually nothing to the fabrication of other goods. In fact, the defense establishment now employs more than half of our best research minds, and in ways that do not contribute directly to the strengthening of the economy; they could be engaged in much more productive and wealth-generating pursuits. Imagine what we could come up with if our best defense thinkers were set to the task of developing flexibly automated factories for the future, which could produce many different types of products for generations to come at competitive prices. Instead, these top minds are put to work developing defense products that in most instances are simply stockpiled until they are declared obsolete and destroyed, and then replaced by other products whose fate is the same.

While we may have twice as many scientists as the Japanese, because of our huge defense establishment we have no more scientists than they do working on purely economic, wealth-producing projects. With a population only half our size, the Japanese have a much higher ratio of civilian engineers per production worker than we do. With so many more engineers per worker, the "thought" content of their products, versus our own, is far higher.

As defense spending outlays increase to a total that will probably surpass $2.1 trillion by the end of Reagan's term, (about $9,500 for each American), there may be momentary gains in jobs, but there will be long-term economic declines throughout the country. First, as already mentioned, the defense buildup has hurt us by diverting our brightest minds. The Pentagon, which accounted for about half of all federally funded research until about 1980, now grabs 74 percent of those research funds. According to the less than dovish *Economist* (August 14, 1987): "the needs of the military are steadily diverging from those of industry at a time when the military is supporting a larger proportion of America's research effort." The defense sector's management style, which emphasizes production first and cost second, is the antithesis of the way the private sector functions, having to pay attention, as it does, to sound business practices.

Second, the arms buildup has contributed enormously to keeping interest rates up since so much of it has been financed through deficit spending. Although we need a strong defense, $2.1 trillion invested in weapons means $2.1 trillion sacrificed from other areas of the economy. Given our current economic condition, the current level of military spending increasingly seems a wild extravagance. Just ask yourself whether at least some of the $9,500 spent on your behalf by former defense secretary Caspar Weinberger wouldn't have been better invested in enhancing our economic competitiveness instead of swelling our debt.

The deleterious effects of overspending on defense and "intellect intensive" defense-related research have recently been pointed out not by an antiwar activist group but by no less an august financial institution than Lloyds Bank of England. In the *Lloyds Review,* three British economists showed that there is an inverse relationship between high military research spending and overall industrial performance.

According to the report by Mary Kaldor, Margaret Sharp, and William Walker, those Western nations that spent the biggest share of their GNPs on military research have now become the least competitive industrially. Since 1979, both Britain and the United States—the two Western powers spending the largest share of their GNPs on military research—have lost significant ground to those countries that put less of their research capabilities into military-related categories. While our overall economic competitive index rating was 99 in 1979, according to the independent Paris-based Organization for Economic Cooperation and Development, the Germans, who spend far less than we do on military research, scored 111.3 and the Japanese, who spend even less, came in at 110.3. Today, because of our excessive military burden, the report says, we have fallen to an even lower competitive index rating of 94.3 while the Germans soared to 128.0 and the Japanese jumped to 138.3. Competitiveness, in this study, is taken to be the excess of economic output over domestic absorptions. That is why Germany and Japan, which produce far more than they consume, score so high.

Other studies confirming the negative impact of defense spending on competitiveness were produced by the New York-based Council on Economic Priorities and by the French Defense Ministry. (France, which spent the third-largest percentage of its GNP on military research of any major industrial power also suffered a drop in its competitiveness rating from 103.5 in 1979 to 100.2 in 1986.)

Another factor intervenes to our detriment. Not only do our recent excessive military expenditures translate into overall economic losses, but the same Lloyds study indicates that, unlike a generation ago, today's military technology is generally far too specialized to offer many useful consumer-sector spinoffs.

It was an acknowledged strategy of the Reagan administration to allocate great sums to defense in an effort to drive the smaller Russian economy into ruin if the Russians tried to keep up with our spending rate. Unfortunately, one unintended side effect of that admirable strategy has been the

further, and future, improverishment of the American people
through the growth of debt and through the theft of some
of our best research minds from the private sector. If we
continue in this vein, rather than attaining mastery over the
Russians, we will end up mirroring them with an equally
moribund economy hamstrung by low productivity and excessive military costs. Already we are beginning to suffer from
some of the familiar Soviet diseases such as bad service, increasingly shoddy goods, and an air travel system that every
day more closely resembles Aeroflot. In other words, the
big-budget, debt-financed Reagan buildup, if continued, may
drive both the Russians and ourselves to ruin.

IN A very short span of time (since about 1980) we have
gone from being the world's most dynamic economy and
its largest creditor to being its greatest importer of foreign
goods and by far its largest debtor. We have witnessed enormous increases in each American's level of personal indebtedness, just as we have seen tremendous hikes in governmental
borrowing. On all levels we are now living far beyond our
means and someday soon we will be held responsible; we
will be compelled to settle our accounts and pay for the
biggest borrowing binge in the history of the world.

We can, of course, resist paying for the enormous buildup
in debt by doing nothing. Yet choosing to do nothing will,
without doubt, serve only to accelerate the existing Decline
and Crash and will lead us almost certainly into a severe,
full-scale depression. If we choose to settle our accounts
through a depression, we will wipe all acounts clean as the
value of assets rapidly falls; all economic activity will cease
to exist in a painful, disruptive, and dangerous reshuffling
of accounts. In a depression, failure to repay loans results
not only in debts that are wiped out, but also in deposits
that are wiped out, since little money flows to the bank to
repay outstanding loans. With rapidly growing numbers of
loan defaults there will be an increased squeamishness on
the part of our overseas creditors, who could demand the

repayment of their considerable loans, sell their U.S. assets, and exchange their dollars for other currencies. Taken together, these domestic and foreign actions would cause a calamity of tremendous proportions not only here but abroad as the entire post–World War II global economy grinds to a halt.

The other way to pay for this great buildup of debt is for the federal government to print money. If it so wishes, the government can print enough money to pay off a large share of its debt. It can also print money and allocate those funds to an otherwise bankrupt FDIC/FSLIC system in an attempt to survive a prolonged period of loan defaults that would otherwise destroy the banking system.

This strategy, which was tried in pre–World War II Germany, and more recently in Argentina, Brazil, Bolivia, and Israel, has always failed. Its objective, to pay back loans, heat up the economy, and thereby stimulate production and growth, has usually instead turned into a short-lived festival of consumption whereby speculators buy and sell gold, silver, diamonds, stocks, bonds, and real estate while the average consumer rushes out to purchase a host of products before prices rise. The ultimate outcome of such an attempt to reheat the economy is a tremendous surge of inflation, more than 1,000 percent in some years in both Argentina and Israel, and a currency with a rapidly plummeting value. An inflationary solution to our debt dilemma is not a solution; it is yet another invitation to international catastrophe and a sure way to further divert funds from productive investment. Increased inflation resulting from a governmental attempt to buy its way out of debt the easy way is sure to destroy not only our own economy (as prices rise out of sight) but also the economies of those countries that have loaned us money, have invested in our nation's potential for growth, or trade with us.

The only way to save our future from even further declines in standard of living is to grow our way out of debt by returning to the level of investment we maintained a generation earlier and by drastically trimming our defense budget so as to redirect creative minds to the consumer sector and to balance the budget to rid ourselves of high interest rates. Barring that, if we are not careful, our economic slide may force us to adopt some of the strategies of much earlier eras when legal and religious edicts prevented the accumulation of debt during times of limited or no income growth.

5

"POCKET PROSPERITY" AND STEADY DECLINE

IT HAS become customary for every aspiring presidential candidate to visit the blighted slums of the South Bronx, the rusting steel mills of Youngstown, and the boarded-up storefronts of Detroit. In front of each of these monuments to our decline, the candidates, Democrat and Republican alike, outline their plans for national renewal and rejuvenation.

In spite of these rituals, the closed factories and boarded-up shops remain as the nation slides down the wage-scale ladder. To visitors from abroad, who have built up their images of America from movies and television (one of the few sectors of the economy where we still have a favorable balance of trade), the reality of life in the United States is staggering. I remember one group of Danish physicians who had come to New York to attend a meeting of the United Nations on the problems of drug addiction. These physicians were so overwhelmed by what they saw on the city's streets that they were nearly speechless. In an interview later in the day they told the various media that they had been warned about New York's urban poverty, drugs, and decay, but that no warnings could have prepared them for the level of devastation that they encountered. For the Danes, a nation we rescued from near destruction after World War II, and for nearly all of Europe, the kind of poverty that exists in the midst of our cities seems like a horrible relic of the past.

Residents of the South Bronx, Youngstown, and Detroit can all remember when their cities were not devastated. They can remember when the businesses in their areas were operating nearly at full capacity in the years just prior to the 1971 onset of the Decline and Crash, but in many cases they cannot understand what has happened—what has made more than 2 million high-paying manufacturing jobs leave the country.

Even though unemployment nationwide is now at about the same level as in 1979, just before the advent of the Reagan revolution, most of the recent job growth has been in the low-paying service sector, as already mentioned. Since 1981 employment in the service sector has grown from 65 million to 75 million, more than a third of the population and almost half of the work force, with the majority of these new jobs centering in retail sales (including fast-food restaurants) and paying between $4.39 and about $5 or $6 per hour for an overall average of about $200 per week, before taxes, for full-time employment. This may be enough to support a teenager living with friends or at home, but certainly not a family.

A large share of these new, low-paying service jobs are only part time and offer few, if any, benefits. In a growing number of cases these jobs do not even offer access to health insurance. According to the Bureau of Labor Statistics, in 1987 there were 5.5 million workers who considered themselves "underemployed"; that is, they had part-time jobs but were seeking, from necessity, full-time jobs. This picture shows the wage and employment shift taking place in this country and it further emphasizes the increased disparity between the nation's rich and poor, a disparity that is rapidly growing.

Barry Bluestone, a professor of economics at Boston College and an expert on income distribution, sees a very dangerous portent for the future if this trend toward an ever greater concentration of wealth increases. According to Bluestone, writing in the February 1, 1987, *New York Times,* with growing inequities and a shrinking middle class, the American Dream itself must be called into question, since even the opportunity of becoming middle class is no longer open to everyone. With entrance to the middle class closed, the level of frustration and despair on the streets of this country can only increase.

Since the late 1960s the United States has not had a period of growth and prosperity that was equally shared among all the different regions of the country. For more than a decade, prosperity in one region has been accompanied by decline in another. Since the late 1970s one or two economic sectors at a time have gained, while others have declined, so there has been no general increase in the overall level of prosperity. This is especially true as the number of jobs in the service sector has grown while the number of jobs in the higher paying production industries has shrunk, leaving large pockets of unemployment and disillusionment in many of our former manufacturing cities.

According to Gar Alperovitz, president of the Washington-based National Center for Economic Alternatives, writing in the 1986 premier issue of *Tikkun,* there has been a "continual circulation of what jobs there are, musical chairs fashion, around America's internal continental empire—so that at one moment New England would be down and the Southwest up, then the Far West down and the South up, and so on." But since the 1960s, overall growth in individual income and wealth has eluded us.

As the nature of the economy has changed, each region has had its ups and downs. In many instances, families have been forced to move gypsy style from city to city simply to stay employed. Seen in a positive light, these regional ups and downs are significant because they reflect the diversity of our vast economy and the varied wealth of the regions. But these regional differences also reflect the fact that the economy as a whole is not performing as well as it once did and that there are pockets of overheated prosperity amid oceans of slow decline.

Recognizing that the problems facing each state reflect more than just the economics of that state, the governors demanded national economic solutions to their problems in both 1986 and 1987. In 1986, in the report released at the National Governors' Convention, the nation's governors stressed the very disturbing fact that thirty-seven of our fifty states were, and continue to be, in the middle of a recession, with the food, raw materials, and manufacturing heartland of the country affected most severely. This heartland is now suffering from unemployment rates far in excess of the national average and from declining urban and rural property and land values. In the 1987 report, the governors again stressed the perilous condition of their states' economies and recommended that the nation as a whole put away its regional rivalries and differences and immediately undertake a massive drive to export American goods and services. As a result of these conferences, individual states like Illinois, California, Texas, New York, and Michigan have all begun to promote their own exports in Europe and Asia, but so far with few results.

Since 1971, only one or two sectors of the economy at a time, and just a couple of regions at a time, have prospered. These mini-booms caused a flurry of activity in one region, complete with rapid, localized wage and employment gains and even rapid real estate development, only to be followed by a mini-bust in which economic activity subsided and much of the area's job and wage gains were lost. Just consider that the average price of a home in Los Angeles, or in southern New England or New York, is nearly triple that of homes in Cleveland, Akron, Indianapolis, or Detroit.

California and the West Coast experienced the first of these post–Decline and Crash mini-boom/mini-bust cycles in 1971 when the aerospace industry, which had grown so quickly during the 1960s as a result of the Vietnam War and the space program, was forced to lay off thousands of engineers, designers, and assembly workers from San Diego to Seattle. Boeing alone laid off 60,000 in the Seattle area. The collapse was so bad that workers lost their jobs and in many cases their homes as well, and an entire generation of college students was dissuaded from studying engineering. This led to a shortage of aerospace engineers just a few years later when business finally picked up. Even when this sector resumed its growth, especially during the period of Reagan's big defense buildup, aerospace manufacturing employment never reached its former levels; employment at Boeing is still 13,000 below its 1969 peak, which reflects an overall increase in the company's operating efficiency but also increased competition from foreign manufacturers at the expense of Boeing and the other American airplane makers. California-based Lockheed, which went bust in 1971 only to be revived by a federal loan, has since gone out of the passenger airplane business completely owing to new and intense competition primarily from European aircraft manufacturers. It has decided to specialize in military and space products, which are government funded, usually limited to American manufacturers, and offer significantly higher profits than civilian sector projects.

The early downturn in the West due to the sharp slump in the aerospace industry is not the only example of how "pocket prosperity" can arise and then decline rapidly, adding to the overall net negative growth in wages that we have been experiencing since the early 1970s. Just consider the way job seekers flocked to Houston in the middle and late 1970s from as far away as Detroit and even New England, egged on by media reports of the demise of the North and the rise of the so-called "sunbelt" states. Houston's boom, which lasted less than a decade, was fueled by OPEC's artificially inflated oil prices, which brought a rush of "petrodollars" into the Texas economy and stimulated new oil exploration at home as well as worldwide. Houston-based companies, which are the world's leading suppliers of oil field equipment, received a tremendous boost from the OPEC price hikes, as the rest of the nation suffered. To take advantage of the growing Texas economy, dozens of companies moved to

Houston thinking they would escape the decay of the North, flee from the high cost of heating their offices during winter, and cash in on the Texas real estate boom. But when the price of oil fell and the media's predictions of the sunbelt's rise were shown to be false, thousands of newly arrived northerners were left without jobs and with highly overvalued real estate that they were unable to sell, even at auction.

During the same period Silicon Valley was also hailed as a mecca for opportunity. In a flush of activity hundreds of new high-tech companies were founded, and again people seeking jobs trekked across the nation. The computer sector soon became saturated as cheap Japanese, Korean, and Taiwanese imports invaded the market just as the major purchasers were curtailing their buying plans in response to the Reagan recession of 1981–1982. Soon Silicon Valley was faced with the same type of calamitous regional slowdown that its new inhabitants had hoped they had left behind. Between 1984 and 1985, 17,000 of Silicon Valley's finest and most highly skilled workers lost their jobs as hundreds of companies were forced to retrench or just go bust. In the face of company closings, plant shutdowns, and a host of jobs migrating overseas, the commercial real estate market in the Silicon Valley collapsed, culminating in a vacancy rate exceeding 35 percent.

Today pocket prosperity can be found in the "frostbelt" region of New York City and New England, an area discounted just a few years ago by the media as being too cold and too old. But this region is not booming as a result of any broad-based production: Its Silicon Highway (Route 128) computer industry has not fully recovered from its slump, and most of the textile mills, shoe factories, and brass foundries have closed. Only the regional defense manufacturers like United Technology Corporation and General Dynamics' Electric Boat Division are booming, as a result of the Reagan arms buildup. The real reason for the region's success is its high concentration of financial institutions and corporate headquarters (employment in New York City alone in the securities and commodities industries has now topped 150,-

ooo, double the figure of a decade ago). And, just like Houston and Silicon Valley before it, the current site of the nation's floating mini-boom is attracting immigrants from around the country, driving up real estate values in Connecticut, Massachusetts, New Jersey, and Long Island, while land values plummet in the Midwest. Yet even as a host of commentators are declaring the health and vitality of the frostbelt it is important to remember that not since 1971 have we been able to sustain rising incomes and increased property values in more than one or at most two regions of the country at the same time. Nor do we yet know the full impact the October 19 stock crash will have on this region so dominated by the financial industry. Moreover, experience has shown that a mini-bust has followed each mini-boom in the Decline and Crash economy, so the overall results have been a continuation of the decline in income and increase in debt.

In a haphazard economy with no future planning, such as ours, it is extremely difficult to produce overall growth. The French, Japanese, and Scandanavian economies, where the governments actively participate in economic planning, have all been growing much faster than the U.S. economy without concentrating wealth and without suffering from a slide in wages. The Japanese in particular have achieved incredible overall growth and have one of the world's most egalitarian distributions of income. Furthermore, the countries that have favored planning have not had the problem of one region rising at the expense of another, which is so characteristic not only of the United States but also of the equally laissez-faire British economy. Britain, like the United States, has shunned any attempt to plan for the future and has seen big growth in one region, London, with severe declines in others.

The pattern of regional boom in the midst of overall decline reflects the unplanned way in which our economy operates. An unplanned economy is not entirely negative. During times of overall prosperity, legions of entrepreneurs can make the most of a climate of expansion and need little, if any, governmental help. But during periods of intense international competition and shrinking markets, the government can help companies and individual firms by offering incentives for companies to enter new and developing markets. During these periods of intense international competition, the government has many ways to stimulate investment and even promote exports. If used correctly, planning can pull companies gently into the future by offering incentives such as loan guarantees, export financing, research subsidies, and tax credits for new investment and for investment in certain regions. The pull method of planning, which has been extremely successful in Japan and Scandanavia, forces no company to do what it does not want to do and contrasts sharply with the strong-arm push method of planning, which is used in the Soviet Union and in other socialist countries to force firms to undertake specific types of work—with poor economic results.

Aside from the rigors of marketing and distribution, which are important but secondary elements of any economy, there are two major beats to the rhythm of any nation's business. These two beats partly explain the mini-boom/mini-bust cycle in our country.

The first beat is short term and entrepreneurial and is manifested in the development of new products, processes, and services and in bringing those new developments into production and to market. The second beat is managerial, and is reflected in how well the needs of the market are satisfied over the long haul and how well the future needs of the marketplace are anticipated. The well-known management consultant Peter Drucker has written extensively about these two elements in the economy.

The U.S. economy has always been bursting with entrepreneurial energy; Americans excel at developing and entering new markets. In less than a decade, American entrepreneurs single-handedly developed the multibillion-dollar, global market for personal computers and software. During the same period, for a more technical market, American entrepreneurs also developed the multibillion-dollar computer-aided design, imaging, and manufacturing industries—and there were other brilliant successes as well in every industry from food processing and biotechnology to the development of ultralight aircraft.

While we excel at the introduction of new products and processes, we do less well at catering to the long-term needs of the market. In fact, many of our problems today stem from our failure to stress the far less glamorous and dramatic managerial beat of the economy and to think and plan for the long term.

The Japanese far outpace us in management but rarely surpass us in initial development of a market. In an effort to guarantee the long-term welfare of their employees and the long-term success of their country, most Japanese companies, and the government itself, have emphasized the managerial aspect of the economy. They have developed long-term strategies for entering existing markets and have composed detailed plans spanning twenty to fifty years for gaining a share of existing markets, usually by introducing new and highly refined versions of existing products and then slowly upgrading those products. They have even begun to plan new cities around specific industries, such as a new information-based city to be built outside of Tokyo where the top minds of Japan's computer and communications industries can work together as well as share ideas after work.

Japanese companies have pursued a plan based on steadily increasing their share of existing markets since the mid-1950s when they first decided to tackle the precision camera and optical goods market. Beginning with crude copies of advanced German cameras like the Leica and the Rolliflex, the Japanese honed their skills by continually upgrading their entries into these markets until their level of quality and technology began to equal that of the Germans and then surpass it. In the span of less than twenty years, utilizing this long-range, managerial approach, the Japanese were able to gain by far the largest share of the worldwide camera and optical goods market, thereby driving the previously dominant Germans to the sidelines. After the Japanese became the primary power in this huge market, they took aim at some of the other existing markets in which they could use

their advanced optical skills. Small copying machines, professional video recording devices, and computerized silicon chip
etching equipment are markets that the Japanese went after
and now dominate. But this time the firms bested by the
Japanese were not German. They were American firms that
failed to keep pace with the slow, steady, unrelenting Japanese
technological and managerial advance. American firms like
Xerox, Ampex, and Fairchild, which had been the pioneers
in their industries, were driven to the sidelines by their failure
to upgrade their research and manufacturing capabilities for
the long term.

There are exceptions, but most American companies are
not in any way long term in their thinking. Planning twenty-
four months ahead is considered long term by most U.S.
companies, whereas the Japanese routinely look five, ten,
and twenty years into the future when developing their approach to entering a market. The decidedly more entrepreneurial orientation of American business, and perhaps even
the American mind, puts us continually in the position of
developing entirely new markets only to lose them to the
Japanese who plot and plan and wait in the wings. Silicon
Valley may rise and fall in a glorious burst of creativity and
the financial services might flourish in New York and New
England, but as these markets mature, our companies tend
to lose out to those Japanese and other foreign companies
that take the long-term view and that have the backing of
their governments.

One very notable and successful managerial company is
IBM, which has made its reputation and based its strategy
on never entering a new market first. Generally, IBM waits
for someone else to play the role of pioneer before it will
attack a market. Once it has entered the market it takes
the decidedly longer term managerial approach of producing
quality products, backing them up with service, and then
continually upgrading those product while, at the same time,
reducing the price until it has gained the largest market share.
IBM waited nearly five years before it jumped into the personal
computer market, but soon after entering that market it be-

came the dominant player. The same is true with its late entry into the mini-computer market and with its recent decision to write its own software.

The long-term markets are almost all managerial and that is where the bulk of the high-wage manufacturing jobs are located and where wringing out greater efficiencies and gaining in productivity mean the most. It is also the sector that adds the biggest share of added value to the economy as a whole, the sector most regionally concentrated (in the Midwest), and the sector currently under the fiercest siege. And as luck would have it, it is the managerial sector that has been targeted by the Japanese, where their commitment to making incremental gains in quality, service, delivery, and support over the long haul pays off in increased market share.

The declines that we have been experiencing both regionally and nationwide as foreign competitors overtake us on the managerial side of the economy cannot be offset by our entrepreneurial expertise. The reason for this is that most pioneering companies, after their initial burst, fail to grow or simply fail as larger, older, managerial companies enter the markets. Just think back a few years to 1983 when the PC computer market was growing rapidly and companies like Osborne, Franklin, Atari, Coleco, Apple, Tandy, Dictaphone, Kaypro, Rainbow, Sinclair, and finally IBM were all making mayhem in the new market. Today, the only remaining companies in the PC market are those that have adopted a managerial approach (as Apple did when it brought in John Scully to replace its founder, Steven Jobs), those that have had long-term managerial strategies all along (such as Tandy and IBM), or those that attack the lower end of the market in a long-term managerial strategy aimed at controlling a bigger share of the market in the next four or five years (such as the inexpensive Korean imports brought in and built up by large manufacturers like Goldstar).

I have mentioned the dichotomy of the managerial and entrepreneurial beats of the economy to emphasize that what is needed today to strengthen ourselves against the momentum of the Decline and Crash is a better balance between these two activities. We need a renewed commitment to the managerial side of the economy. Though it is perhaps beneficial for a small entrepreneurial company to be merged with a stronger, better run managerial firm, the current takeover craze has a highly negative effect on the long-term viability of the managerial economy. Because takeover artists have forced many of our major companies into shifting from long-term productive investments to buying back their own stock shares and selling off company divisions to raise cash, they have done a great disservice to the economic health of the country. These defensive strategies, which are expensive wastes of resources, only accelerate the Decline and Crash economy by making us less competitive as a nation.

Just consider how ludicrous, destructive, and irresponsible GE's recent purchase of RCA has been to the managerial economy in light of recent events. In 1986, GE, now the nation's second largest defense contractor, purchased RCA from its stockholders for $6.4 billion—the largest non-oil company merger in the United States. GE's chairman John Welch called the takeover a "historic reunification" because the two companies had been one until they were broken up in the 1920s. The business press wrote of the complementarities of the two newly joined companies and of how this newly merged giant would be able to fend off the Japanese challenge by resurrecting America as a superpower in consumer electronics. GE's purchase of RCA was financed with cash and by issuing bonds, which increased this otherwise well-managed company's level of debt.

During the early months of the merger it was hinted that RCA would revamp and modernize its U.S.-based manufacturing facilities, located primarily in the Midwest. This hope was further strengthened when GE broke off its long-term agreement to import Japanese televisions from Matsushita Electric Industries owing to the rise in the value of the yen against the dollar. A modernized U.S. manufacturing capability could even bring production of VCRs, camcorders, and other equipment to our shores, thereby creating a renaissance in U.S. electronics manufacturing, since currently none of these big-ticket consumer items is made domestically.

After having surveyed Japanese and Korean electronics manufacturing plants, a team of American engineering and manufacturing consultants delivered to GE what seemed like very good news: If existing U.S. production facilities were upgraded, they could easily become the world's most efficient and low-cost producers of TVs, beating even the Japanese, Koreans, and Taiwanese. Because GE is also a manufacturer of factory automation equipment, analysts thought such a move to resurrect consumer electronics production in the United States might be an advertisement for GE's automation prowess. In fact, analysts thought it might even start a significant trend among other companies to bring their overseas production back home (the only other U.S. manufacturer of TVs is Zenith, but the amount done in the United States represents only a small share of Zenith's overall manufacturing, which is done primarily in Mexico for TVs and in Japan for computers).

In a surprising move that illustrates the long-term destructiveness of takeovers, GE decided that rather than risk manufacturing domestically, it would sell off both the RCA and GE consumer electronics lines to Thomson, the giant European electronics company owned by the French government, for $500 million in cash and Thomson's medical electronics division in trade. The decision to sell the GE and RCA consumer electronics lines to the French government is surprising in view of the information the company received regarding its prospects for low-cost domestic manufacturing. However, it also illustrates what is now the conventional way companies pay for their aquisitions: They sell off vital production capacity to raise enough cash to retire the debt built up in the takeover transaction. These actions of accumulating debt and selling off divisions to pay for that debt have created what many pundits now call the "hollow corporation," that is, companies that no longer produce anything.

For the time being, Thomson TVs destined for the U.S. market will continue to be made at RCA plants in the Midwest and they will probably also carry the RCA and GE names.

But Thomson is a French company owned by a government that is considered to be a very shrewd economic planner. Putting this American company in the hands of the French government will put workers in Indiana or Ohio at the service of another nation. Not only that, but if there is ever a need to employ out-of-work Frenchmen in Lyons, Paris, or Toulouse, they will most likely take precidence over their American counterparts (French unemployment is much higher than our own). The same is true in terms of upgrading the technology of the American plants. If the Parisian parent company desires to export more TVs from its French factories, investment in Europe will in all likelihood come at the expense of investment in the United States, leaving American workers to make do with less sophisticated technology. And Thomson will have gained the GE and RCA distribution and service networks, enabling it to enter the U.S. market easily with an entire range of products built overseas, thereby further damaging our balance-of-payments picture. So much for the "historic reunification" of GE and RCA.

One of the reasons for preserving our managerial economy has to do with more than simply the health of one or two companies; it has to do with the long-term health of the nation. The reason it is crucial at this juncture to ensure the strength of the manufacturing sector is that we are entering an era of increased competition and chronic oversupply, not just with respect to manufactured goods, but to commodities as well.

At the same time that our managerial companies are besieged by governmental planners in Europe, the managerial-minded Japanese, and the predatory takeover specialists, our economy is becoming increasingly vulnerable to this oversupply of manufactured goods and commodities. It is one of history's more interesting footnotes to recall that a century ago, when Karl Marx predicted capitalism's final crisis, he said that the collapse of our system would be brought about not by shortages but by oversupply. Conditions of oversupply, in market economies, can bring about a galloping deflation during which the value of physical assets plunges.

We have already seen the value of farm assets fall in the Midwest as it faces a run of bad luck: falling prices for agricultural commodities and increased competition in the manufacturing fields. Today, American manufacturers are using barely 78 percent of our manufacturing capacity, which means that factory assembly lines are idle 22 percent of the time. The Midwest, with its high concentration of manufacturing companies, based largely around automobile production, is still reeling from the steady growth of imports.

This region also must endure intense competition from the heavily indebted third world, which is selling off its commodities at bargain basement prices in an effort to pay the interest on a staggering $1 trillion in outstanding loans. The dumping of raw material exports on the world's already flooded commodities market has caused the prices for most commodities to drop to their lowest levels in years. But since these heavily indebted developing countries must use their dwindling export earnings to pay back their loans, they are scarcely able to continue importing our manufactured goods. The loss of the third world as a major importer of American goods has meant the loss of 1.4 million jobs in the manufacturing sector, according to Stuart Tucker of the Washington-based Overseas Development Council, writing in *Policy Focus* (No. 7, 1985). Furthermore, with so much of the world's purchasing power wiped out as the third world struggles with its burden of debt, the problem of manufacturing plant overcapacity is exaggerated not only at home, but in other countries as well. Managing in an environment of increased competition and a shrinking market places greater demands on our managers and requires that they exercise a great deal of precision in formulating their strategies.

According to the comprehensive annual *World Economic Survey* for 1986, produced by the United Nations, since 1985 the third world debtor countries have lost 30 percent of their buying power as a result of the drop in commodity prices occasioned by the current level of oversupply. This 30 percent drop translates into a loss of purchasing power of about $94 billion. Because we are the largest single exporter to the third world (as well as the largest importer of its products), the poor economic health of these countries has hurt us as well and caused us to run a balance-of-payments deficit with the region as a whole. If the third world were purchasing our products in the same quantities as they once did, it is conceivable that their purchases might even offset a significant share of our purchases from Japan. Yet according to the 1987 *World Economic Survey*, there is nothing to indicate that the third world will recover its purchasing power in the foreseeable future since the condition of oversupply is likely to last a good many years.

For the commodity-producing states in the agricultural and mineral belts of the country (the Midwest and sunbelt, primarily), the future is clouded owing to the continued commodities dumping of the third world debtor countries. And since mineral and agricultural producers are among the nation's biggest debtors, the banks that have loaned out funds to these businesses are in trouble. In Nebraska, for example, the value of farmland has dropped 55 percent since 1984. To the typical midwestern banker with a large agricultural portfolio, the drop in the value of farmland represents a disastrous plunge in the backing for those loans and has led to a spate of foreclosures and even farm auctions. This situation is exactly the same for banks that have made loans to oil producers both at home and in the third world. These bankers saw a huge decrease in the value of the backing of these loans as the price of oil slumped from $38 per barrel in 1985 to $10 per barrel in early 1986 before climbing back up to nearly $20 per barrel today. Taken together, the oversupply of commodities and agricultural goods is bringing on a serious deflation of physical assets, particularly in the heart of the country. What's more, since so many loans made to farmers and to oil producers are going bad, and since so much collateral is about to be put on the auction block, the price of these once-valuable assets has nowhere else to go but farther down (8 percent of the nation's 650,000 farms are saddled with debt/equity ratios of 70 percent or greater). According to Mark Drabenstott of the Federal Reserve Bank of Kansas City, as quoted in the June 9, 1986, *BusinessWeek*, the current huge farm debt ratio means widespread farm bankruptcies, with as much as 15 percent of all farm assets soon to be put up for sale.

And then what? In other countries where oversupply is crippling the incomes of the oil producers and farmers there are laws to prevent the sale of those assets, especially to foreigners. But in the United States we have no such laws. With the value of the dollar at an all-time low against a number of other currencies and with so much property on the auction block, it will soon be a very attractive investment for foreigners to purchase our farmland and perhaps even our petroleum reserves.

Just as these gluts are causing downward shifts in the prices for commodities, they are also creating havoc among the manufacturers that cater to the markets. Producers of farm, mining, and oil-field equipment are all suffering in the depressed markets. International Harvester has gone bankrupt only to be resurrected as the newly formed, newly scaled back Navistar; John Deere has not gone bankrupt, but is limping along in a depressed market just after having invested hundreds of millions of dollars in a state-of-the-art automated factory; the giant heavy equipment maker Caterpillar, in an effort to keep production costs low, has shifted much of the manufacturing of its smaller tractors to Korea; and Ford has scaled back its tractor production operations while the big forward-looking Japanese manufacturers like Komatsu have begun their invasion of the farm equipment market.

The remaining parts of the Midwest economy are linked quite tightly either to the automobile industry or to the metals and primary products industries. The auto industry, while considerably healthier than during the 1981 recession, has not recovered fully in terms of employment, nor have wages recovered from the givebacks of that period. One bright spot, however, is the Chrysler Corporation, which recently purchased American Motors from Renault, the automaker owned by the French government. Chrysler also recently announced its intention to export American-built cars to Europe, something that U.S. manufacturers have not attempted for generations.

The midwestern heartland of the country has begun to be known as the "deflation" belt because of the drastic declines in the value of its physical assets (farmland, mines, and commodities) and because of the drop in price of its real estate. Midwestern wages are also falling, especially in the metals sector (the nation's unionized copper mine workers have had to accept a 30 percent wage cut), and agricultural incomes have been in a slump since the failed attempt at a farm strike in 1984 when farmers blocked Washington traffic with their tractors.

Commodity price decreases have been the major culprit behind the drop in the value of physical assets. But the commodity slump has also been responsible for keeping inflation low by offsetting price increases elsewhere in the economy with declines in the prices for raw materials and agricultural products.

A representative sample of price declines includes a 25 percent dip in the price of pork bellies; a one-third decline in the price of wheat; a nationwide 15 percent slump in farmland prices (worse by far in the wheat, corn, and soybean belts); and substantial declines, up to two thirds, in the price of a broad band of metals, minerals, and energy supplies, including coal, oil, iron, copper, and bauxite. Tin prices have dropped so much that trading has been suspended. The collapse in farm and commodity prices is not unique to the United States, though; it is occurring worldwide.

According to John Rutledge, who heads the Claremont Economics Institute in California, as quoted in the June 9, 1986, *BusinessWeek,* there has already been a significant erosion in the overall value of our nation's tangible assets as a result of the deflationary spiral beginning to affect the country. In 1985, our hard assets (farms, homes, factories, and roads) were worth about $12 trillion, which translates into a net worth of about $50,000 for every American. But today, because of the deflation gripping the nation, in particular the Midwest, the value of those assets has dropped by about $1 trillion, with farmers absorbing a disproportionately large part of that decline. According to Rutledge, this drop in the value of our assets will continue as the economy tries to shake out the inflation of the 1970s. If the surge in home equity loans and second mortgages is factored in, the drop in assets will be even larger. To this drop in the value of our assets, add another $1 trillion decline in the value of stocks in October 1987 and the decreased purchasing power of a devalued dollar.

If the deflation proceeds in an orderly way, there is little cause for alarm. Some of the reckless, inflationary policies of Presidents Johnson, Nixon, Ford, and Carter may finally be washed aside. The paper economy would gradually deflate into one based on real, hard assets, and prices would fall, making productive investments far more attractive.

But a rapid deflation, such as one occasioned by a long-term drop in stock prices, will exert a tremendous downward pressure on prices and wages making it very difficult, if not impossible, for the nation's countless debtors to pay back their loans, since both individual and corporate earnings will be greatly reduced. And as the deflationary spiral widens to encompass more than the Midwest, as other areas of the nation are subjected to large-scale oversupply, the problems will really mount. For instance, the commercial real estate sector is now hugely overbuilt and largely financed by money from the nation's pension funds and insurance policies. Severe drops in the value of those assets and stocks, as the oversupply adjusts to the reality of the market, would wipe out a good portion of the nation's retirement funds. It would also make it easier than ever for the rich Japanese and Europeans to purchase U.S. farms, real estate, and companies.

The only policy tool available to stop a deflationary collapse is to reheat the economy by printing money, as I have already mentioned. This strategy, which economists usually call "floating the ship off the rocks," is inflationary and can push the economy toward instability, cause interest rates to climb, discourage productive investment, and cause the value of the dollar to sink. It is an extremely difficult policy to follow because we lack precise methods for controlling the growth of money. And galloping inflation would also rage in the rest of the world, causing the kind of global upheaval that brings with it a great degree of social instability and finally collapse. But with the Federal Reserve Board more nervous about inflation than deflation, it is unlikely that such a policy will ever be attempted.

WITHOUT a smoothly functioning managerial economy, America in the later 1980s and the 1990s will almost certainly suffer a rapid acceleration of the Decline and Crash. With the third world sidelined and its purchasing power dwindling, the remaining markets for goods will be severely overcrowded. As market conditions become more difficult, with far more producers fighting for their dwindling shares of the pie, an interesting phenomenon is likely to occur: Companies that wish to remain in a crowded market will only be able to do so by lowering their prices. To do this, they will be forced to increase the quantity of goods they produce to take full advantage of the economies of scale. This increase of low-cost goods, of course, will just flood markets even more, ensuring that the only firms to survive those conditions will be those that have the most capital and the best management.

Today those firms are almost entirely Japanese. These firms are already proving the value of their long-range managerial expertise by surviving and prospering even with the devaluation of the dollar and the resulting 40 percent appreciation of the yen. Faced with this 40 percent increase, the big Japanese firms were still able to profit handsomely by cutting manufacturing costs by as much as 20 percent, shaving their overhead, lowering their profit margins, and increasing their productivity. Because they were well prepared for this eventuality, having planned for it years before and having wisely saved and invested their massive trade surpluses, they were able to sail through the drastic appreciation of their currency while losing almost no market share in the United States or around the world.

So which firms will be better able to navigate through a period of overcrowded markets and commodity gluts? American firms, which are encumbered by massive levels of debt because they have sold off many of their productive assets to fight takeovers and have failed to invest in productivity-enhancing measures? American companies that are saddled with a group of managers more interested in the value of the stock than in the products they produce? American firms that must contend with a government that is philosophically opposed to planning, competes with them for capital, and is concentrating the talents of its best research brains on noncompetitive military applications? Or the cash-rich, highly productive Japanese companies that have been run by people who have been thinking long term, investing heavily, and working hard to upgrade their products? Japanese companies aided by a "pull"-oriented government-planning agency, years of low interest rates, and almost no military research programs to steal minds from the civilian projects?

At present, the answer is obvious, and we have precious little time to change it.

6

THE THIRD WORLD MOVES NEXT DOOR

LET us take a deeper look at the third world and its impact on our own nation and on our economic decline.

We Americans have never really known just how to regard the third world. At best it is thought of, if it is thought of at all, as a kind of barking dog clamoring for our attention as we concern ourselves with the business of confronting the Soviets or running the world economy. To many Americans, the third world is a hodgepodge of needy, poor people and greedy leaders beginning somewhere just to the south of us.

While it's true that the third world is a frustrating place often easier to ignore than figure out, its importance is growing. It is a region of the world more like a bog that swallows all our good intentions and where, at present, only a small handful of countries have any hope of making it. It is at the same time economically dependent and a new source of competition, a place where countries that receive our aid trounce our own manufacturers in the marketplace. A case in point is Korea, which still receives massive contributions of foreign and military assistance from Uncle Sam, is slowly cornering the PC market with its IBM clones, has made a large dent in the low end of the auto market with the Hyundai line of cars, is beginning to outmaneuver our big civil engineering and construction firms for lucrative contracts in foreign countries, is gaining an increasing share of our home electronics market, and is winning a growing segment of the auto parts and components market. And in spite of billions of dollars of U.S. aid and U.S. troops stationed on its soil, Korea's major imports come not from the United States but from Japan.

The third world is also a region where we have suffered our most humiliating defeats and managed to wrest only the most meager of victories; it is here that the East-West conflict is dragged from the realm of ideology and propaganda to the field of battle. Just consider that in each of the current wars in the third world—in Africa, Asia, Latin America, and the Middle East—the Soviet Union and the United States are supplying, training, bankrolling, and otherwise helping opposing sides. And in the latest and bloodiest of the third world's conflicts, the war between Iran and Iraq, we are once again in the middle, with many American lives already lost.

The third world may occupy us economically and politically, but it has yet to truly enter our consciousness, except as an exotic location in a movie. And yet, the third world is more intimately linked to the United States than to any other major industrial power. Even with so much at stake, it would be difficult to find an American who can name just six or seven third world countries or identify their flags flying outside the United Nations. Magazines like *South* that focus on third world topics and sell in very large numbers in Europe barely make it to the newsstands in America. Even books like former German chancellor Willy Brandt's *North South* and *Common Crisis,* concerning the relationships between rich and poor countries, hardly sell in the American market but make it to the best-seller lists in Britain and in Europe.

We ignore the third world partly because, unlike the Europeans, we have no real history as a colonial power; we happened on the scene too late to snatch up any colonies. True, for a brief period we owned the Philippines and Cuba, but these came to us relatively recently as prizes from our war with Spain, not as lands we settled. For nearly four hundred years France, Britain, Spain, Portugal, Belgium, and the Netherlands involved themselves with the third world in a highly intimate, often cruel, and always complicated series of relationships. During this time these countries honed their specialized diplomatic skills and learned the subtle art of dividing to conquer. The Europeans may have been the colonizers and exploiters, responsible for centuries of repressive colonial rule, but somehow the United States bumbled its way into being perceived as the "enemy" while a nation like Holland, with its brutal history in Indonesia and Suriname, is now considered to be "like-minded" by the same third world countries it controlled well beyond the end of World War II. And France, which was at one time the world's leading slave trader, controlled Algeria, and fought viciously in Vietnam just before we entered the war, has continued to remain on excellent terms with its former colonies both in Indochina and in Africa.

Emotionally, we have also tended to identify with the colony, rather than the colonizer, but in a rather curious way. Instead of supporting wars of national liberation we have generally been on the side of the powers that be, forsaking negotiation while arguing that stability, in the third world, is a far more important prerequisite to the creation of wealth than is equality. In no other region of the globe have we behaved less pragmatically or more ideologically. We have tolerated, for example, Russian domination in Eastern Europe and the rise of both socialism and strong Communist parties in Western Europe. But in the third world, we have often supported the most unpopular regimes, and reaped universal scorn for having done so. While we have fared beautifully in our postwar relationships with Europe and Japan—becoming allies with our former enemies—we have made one costly blunder after another in the third world, all the time failing to grasp the importance of that region and the three-quarters of humanity that reside there.

Consider that since World War II our only wars have been in third world countries: Korea, Laos, Lebanon, the Dominican Republic, Cuba, Vietnam, Cambodia, and Grenada. We are currently in the middle of a conflict between Iran and Iraq, backing the Contras in Nicaragua, and working with the government of El Salvador to end its civil war. Our chief post–Vietnam War humiliations came not from Europe or the Soviet Union, but from third world Iran, which captured our embassy, and our largest post-Vietnam troop losses came from the deaths of 242 marines on a peacekeeping mission in third world Lebanon. Libya, which we bombed, and which cost two American lives, is also a third world country, as is Syria, the home of world terrorism.

We are not doing much better with the third world economically. For more than a decade we were held hostage in effect by OPEC, composed entirely of third world countries, over the price of oil. The tremendous increases in the price of oil still haunt us: the weakening of our banking system precipitated by the increase in Latin American debt occasioned by our banks' bitter need to recycle OPEC's vast deposits of petrodollars.

Although it is now beginning to change, most of the third world still sustains itself on the export of raw materials to developed countries. With the exception of a handful of so-called NICs, for "newly industrialized countries" (comprising South Korea, Taiwan, Hong Kong, Singapore, Malaysia, and Brazil), that are linked to American, European, and Japanese multinational companies, most of the third world has been in a profound state of decline for the last six or seven years.

The reasons for the declines in the standards of living in these geographically disparate countries are quite similar. First, although these countries have grown economically since

gaining independence from their former rulers, their populations have also grown at astounding rates. Kenya, for example, may have grown at 5 percent over the last year in economic terms, but with a population increase of 4 percent
per year most of the benefits from that economic growth
are negated.

Second, because the majority of developing countries are
raw materials exporters, they have suffered dramatically from
a downturn in the prices of these commodities. The collapse
in the tin market, the fall in the price of rubber and aluminum,
the oversupply of oil, and the shrinking market for such
natural products as jute and sisal have left many developing
countries unable to pay their bills. According to the 1986
report of the independent United Nations Committee for
Development Planning, the drop in oil prices has hit a number
of developing countries especially hard: "The fall in the price
of oil has benefitted many, but is having a devastating effect
on a few major developing countries, notably Nigeria and
Mexico." The significance of Mexico's and Nigeria's fall is
especially important to us, not just because Mexico is our
neighbor and Nigeria is a pro-Western ally as well as black
Africa's most populous nation. These two countries are vital
to our interests because they are our two largest suppliers
of imported oil and were big purchasers of our export goods.
They are also two of the third world's largest debtor countries,
a fact which has direct impact on the health of our banks.

One factor affecting the developing African nations specifically, which has so far not harmed the other third world
countries, has been the progressive droughts and severe distur-
bance of the environment over the last decade. This deterioration of the ecosystem is bad enough to be labeled a "break-
down of the biosystem threatening its capacity to support
life," Lester Brown, president of the World Watch Institute,
told me. Africa, with its rapidly growing population and
drought-induced famine, has experienced falling per-capita
incomes for more than a decade, and this trend is accelerating.
Between 1980 and 1986, per-capita income has declined by
more than 12 percent in the sub-Saharan region, with the

overall effect that "low income Africa is now poorer than in 1960," Brown said. The erosion of what wealth there was in Africa and the continued hardships that must be endured have also increasingly strained the political balance between moderate and radical forces and weakened Western interests.

What makes Africa's fall to a pre-1960 standard of living so bitterly discouraging is that it means conditions were actually better in Africa during colonial rule than under self-rule. According to the World Bank, more declines are expected in the drought-affected regions of Africa, and with those declines will come more political chaos.

But the most devastating, and negative, impacts on the developing countries occurred during the heyday of OPEC, from 1973 to 1983, when oil prices shot up tenfold. Just consider that most developing countries import both oil and manufactured goods. For these countries, the increased price of oil represented a severe strain on their balance of payments. In 1980, for example, the non–oil-exporting developing countries had a balance-of-payments deficit with OPEC of more than $86 billion, which jumped to $99 billion in 1981. At the same time, the countries that export manufactured goods to these third world nations raised their prices in an attempt to compensate for higher oil costs, when inflation was rampant, further contributing to the high prices for these manufactured goods. Countries that imported both manufactured products and oil were doubly hit by the sudden, huge increases in costs.

Through intense restraint, which meant resorting to tight fiscal policies and tolerating high levels of unemployment, the developed countries, led by the United States, were able to bring their accounts roughly in balance with OPEC's by 1981. Fiscal restraint meant that interest rates shot up to levels as high as 18 percent, which threw the developed nations into recession and, according to the 1986 report of the United Nations Committee for Development Planning, caused the world economy to "crash." By 1982, world industrial production had contracted by 4 percent, exports from the developed world had plunged 18.5 percent, and protectionism was on the rise because of high unemployment. In the United States the White House imposed "voluntary restraints" upon Japanese auto exports and other countries did much the same. While "voluntary" restraints were sufficient in Europe and the United States, in the developing countries it was not, and per-capita income fell for the third year in a row. Faced with declining export markets, a large group of developing countries had no recourse but to borrow funds to keep their economies afloat and to continue to import vital energy stocks. By 1983, forty developing countries had problems servicing their accumulated debt.

Oil-importing developing countries like Brazil, Argentina, and Zaire were not the only ones to accumulate large external debts. Mexico, Nigeria, Indonesia, Ecuador, and Venezuela each outlined ambitious development plans based on the promise that oil would sell indefinitely on the world market at $38 per barrel or higher. Banks, eager to lend the petrodollars they had on deposit at record high interest rates, leapt at the opportunity to channel money to these oil-rich developing nations. Figuring loan collateral as the amount of oil left in the ground at $38 per barrel and up, our shortsighted international banks ignored warnings and simply assumed they could go on making oil-assured loans forever. The heady confidence of the late 1970s and early 1980s led banks and third world governments into a deception of the blind leading the blind. Banks, believing that present conditions would last well into the future, let the money flow until the third world was awash in debt beyond its ability to repay even at record levels for each barrel of oil. The third world, drunk on its newfound riches, borrowed without restrain and spent lavishly.

By the mid-eighties, at the end of the oil boom, the indebtedness of developing countries had assumed vast proportions, exceeded only by the level of debt of the United States. Mexico alone owes more than $100 billion, Brazil owes even more, and Argentina is not far behind. All developing countries, taken as a group, now owe nearly $1 trillion, an astonishing figure, equal to about $1,000 per person in a region with average annual incomes of less than $400 per person per year.

One important and very dangerous indicator of how this enormous debt affects the developing countries is called the debt-service ratio, which is the percentage of income earned from exports that must go to pay back the interest—not the principal—on the debt. The figures from the United Nations indicate that, over all, debtor developing countries now spend more than half of their export earnings servicing their debts, with some, like Mexico and Brazil, spending considerably more. Tragically, although the majority of developing-country export income now goes to pay back loans, little of that loan money either benefited the countries or remained there.

Unfortunately, there is another side to the collusion between U.S., European, and Japanese banks and the governments of the third world that has complicated the debt crisis even more. According to New York-based economist James S. Henry, more than half of the money originally loaned to the third world was siphoned off by corrupt leaders and redeposited in our banks under their names in the form of "flight capital." Writing in the April 14, 1986, *New Republic,* Henry states that in Mexico alone 575 people were named as having U.S. bank accounts of $1 million or more—politicians, police chiefs, labor leaders, and so on—at a time when the Mexican government was going to the U.S. Treasury in hopes of borrowing a further $6 billion to $10 billion to meet its interest payments.

By awarding huge contracts to relatives and friends, third world leaders were able to seize funds earmarked for their countries. Many big projects seem to have been conceived simply as neat ways to put money borrowed by the government in private pockets. Henry quotes Jack Anderson, who says Mexican president Miguel de la Madrid may have deposited as much as $162 million into a private Swiss bank account in 1983, at a time when Mexican unemployment topped 30 percent and, according to Henry, average real wages plummeted to 1962 levels.

In 1981, when Mexico accumulated $20 billion in new debt, capital flight may have amounted to as much as $11 billion. In Venezuela, another big oil-producing debtor nation, capital flight may have actually equaled loans to the country, while in Argentina 60 percent of those loans left home.

So much money landing in the accounts of the elite of the third world could not have escaped our bankers' attention. After all, often the same bank both made the loan and accepted the deposit. While there is nothing new in this kind of corruption, it is surprising that during the heyday of third world lending no one blew the whistle on what may have been the largest heist in history. Ethics being what they are, many of our bankers not only turned a blind eye to where their loans ended up, but actively (and cynically) courted these third world millionaires to utilize their services and invest in their schemes.

At best, under these conditions, only about half the money loaned to the developing world was put to good use. The great development projects that these loans were supposed to bankroll have been either killed or curtailed. Without these wealth-producing projects, neither the lot of the third world multitudes will improve nor will our banks be repaid.

While we may disdain the third world for what we regard as its mismanagement of funds, corruption, inefficiency, human rights abuses, and contempt for the West, it still exerts a heavy influence on our lives. For example, after Canada and Japan, our largest balance-of-payments deficits are not with the rich European countries, but with the third world. We now import more from Mexico and a few of the NICs, Taiwan, Korea, and Hong Kong, than we do from Britain, Germany, France, and Italy combined. And these soaring imports are further weakening the structure of our economy.

Increasingly, our imports from the third world are in the form of manufactured goods from the NICs. This has been occurring because we have been steadily shifting our production facilities to the third world and then importing the products. Electronics, automobiles and replacement parts, textiles and shoes, and even sophisticated high-tech products like audio equipment, VCRs, and computers and computer chips, come increasingly from the third world NICs. Our investment in these countries has been large and now the fruit of that investment is coming back to haunt us in the form of low-priced imports that compete directly with our own struggling domestic industries. According to the Washington-based Overseas Development Council (*Policy Focus,* No. 7, 1985), "the United States now consumes a remarkable 60 percent of the third world's exports and manufactures. Developing countries account for 43 percent of the mammoth U.S. trade deficit."

Prosperity in the South, the latest fashionable name for the 110-odd countries of the third world, is vital to prosperity in the North, and especially to the economic health of North America. This is true not simply because we have lent the South much money and because so many of our multinational corporations have located their production facilities there, but because the South has emerged as one of our biggest export markets. For instance, the deep recession in the third world that has been going on for the last six years, precipitated by the debt crisis, has meant a substantial loss of jobs in the U.S. export sector, as many as 1.4 million between 1980 and 1984, according to Overseas Development Council economist Stuart Tucker, writing in *Policy Focus,* (No. 7, 1985).

For good or ill, the relationship between the South and the United States is deeply interdependent. Because of our own history of investment overseas, we now import a great deal from the third world. When RCA builds a large communications satellite, for example, it may use silicon chips produced by its Malaysian affiliate instead of chips made in the United States, thus contributing to Malaysia's rise from obscurity to the third largest producer of integrated circuit components in the world and one of the primary electronics manufacturers, just behind Japan and the United States.

But the issue is more than just chips. Caterpillar is now

building its smaller earth mover tractors in Korea. Meanwhile, one of Caterpillar's domestic rivals, Clark Equipment Company, has just signed a deal to import the small forklift trucks it once built domestically from the Korean manufacturing giant Samsung Heavy Industries. This is happening just as Ford has begun importing Korean-built cars, American Volkswagen has begun importing Brazilian cars, and Chrysler has decided to put Mexican-made engines in some of its cars and join the ranks of the hundreds of American manufacturers that are jettisoning their domestic plants in favor of facilities in the South—all contributing to the loss of U.S. manufacturing jobs.

In Mexico alone, General Motors employs more than 24,000 people (roughly the number of assembly workers GM laid off in 1986). GM's Mexican employees are making parts for U.S. models as well as for GM's Mexican-produced cars (soon to be sold in the United States) at wages usually below $1 per hour, a fraction of the salaries paid in Detroit. RCA, Zenith, Westinghouse, Chrysler, General Electric, and others employ an estimated 85,000 Mexican workers along the border region alone in the *maquiladora* program whereby U.S. parts are shipped south of the border for assembly in Mexican factories and then shipped back to the United States for further assembly, packaging, and shipping to customers here at home. And while American companies take advantage of joint U.S.-Mexican sponsorship of the *maquiladora* program, with its bilateral agreement to move machinery and products between the two countries duty free, Japanese companies, like Hitachi, have started to locate their assembly plants along the Mexican border and assemble products there destined for the United States. In this way, Hitachi hopes to avoid paying U.S. import fees by selling to the U.S. market through its Mexican subsidiary.

Rock-bottom wages and little concern for the environment or for working conditions make Mexico, and other third world nations, attractive places in which to invest. Many of these countries, eager for investment, also offer other incentives such as a decade or more free of taxes and years of duty-free imports for the investor company. These tax "holidays," as they are called, can even be extended to include pollution and safety "holidays" during which time the government of the third world country allows manufacturing operations without pollution controls, even for toxic waste, and assembly operations without regard for common safety concerns. In this way, an American (or European) company can produce goods that would be outlawed at home and still claim that it operates in violation of no nation's law.

In December 1986, General Motors announced it would cut 24,200 jobs from its U.S. manufacturing facilities while AT&T announced that it would cut 29,000 from its manufacturing ranks and close several U.S. factories. What was left unsaid in both instances was that these jobs would ultimately be going overseas to subsidiaries or affiliates in third world countries. While there is nothing wrong with shipping some of our low-level manufacturing jobs overseas—if they are replaced by new jobs in the growing high-tech areas of the manufacturing economy—there is no evidence thus far that these lost jobs will be replaced by anything more than low-paying service sector employment.

The real problem with shifting our manufacturing facilities to the third world is that this move contributes to a powerful structural change in American business that alters the very fabric of the economy while, at the same time, institutionalizing many of our worst problems. The failure of the Reagan administration to halt the embarrassing and highly damaging balance-of-payments deficits, over $175 billion in 1986 alone despite the tremendous drop in the value of the dollar, relates to a U.S. economy dominated by multinational companies that increasingly have shifted production overseas. In the process, these multinationals have transformed themselves from producers of goods to importers and marketers of goods made overseas by their foreign divisions and affiliates. Because so many of our imports come to us in the form of trade between the different divisions of American multinationals, the balance-of-payments deficit has become structurally integrated into the economy. This means that the trade deficit will be extremely hard to reverse for two major reasons.

First, if Chrysler specifies Mexican engines for its cars that means that every Chrysler automobile sold will contribute negatively to the balance of payments of this country since it will contain a large number of imported components. The decision to include foreign components in our domestically manufactured goods—or, increasingly, domestically assembled goods—is not something that can be changed overnight or taken lightly, especially if those imported components are as complicated and as expensive as automobile engines.

To produce these engines, whether in Detroit, Korea, or Mexico, requires a significant investment in technology and in real estate. Money must also be spent to train managers and workers, build communication and shipping facilities, and monitor production. These investments, which can total in the tens or even hundreds of millions of dollars, require a substantial amount of time to amortize, as much as twenty years in some cases.

Because of the heavy investment and long-term commitment required to begin offshore manufacturing, companies are very reluctant to cancel these plans. The instances of companies moving their production from the third world back to the United States are extremely rare—GM's bold decision to move some of its Delco auto radio production from Singapore back to the states to take advantage of U.S. advances in automation is one notable exception. What's more, as overseas manufacturing becomes more integrated into a company's overall operations, the company gets used to paying labor costs that are only a fraction of what the typical American worker makes. Organizationally, the company gets used to the idea that manufacturing is done far from the headquarters office and that it is therefore less important than the financial manipulations of its principal officers. Finally, as offshore manufacturing becomes a way of life for a company, the cost of moving production back to our shores jumps dramatically, especially when new real estate and technology must be purchased.

The second big problem with offshore production is that

it sets up opposition between the interests of our country and those of the corporation. While the competitiveness of a country depends on what happens within its borders, the competitiveness of a company is based on what happens within its organizational structure, which may take advantage of different circumstances in different countries. Dispensing with domestic production integrates the importation of manufactured goods into the national economy. American companies that can sell their imported products cheaper than their American products will do so in an attempt to gain market share, but by doing this they will continue to force down American wages while they add to our already huge trade deficit. In this way, the fight for market share among our companies, and the need those companies have to sell cheaper products, will only serve to institutionalize our decline by making both the wage slide and the trade deficits permanent features of the economy.

The negative impact on the nation's balance of trade occurs when a company imports products either from its wholly owned foreign subsidiary or from a company in which it does not have ownership. If Zenith imports televisions from its Mexican plant, it still must pay for the costs of producing those sets abroad with the money it receives from the American purchasers of those sets. A significant share of the money spent on the purchase of a Mexican-made Zenith set sold in Chicago will end up leaving the country even though Zenith may own a large share of its Mexican affiliate. The same is true if a Korean-made Goldstar set is sold in Chicago—American money will still be fleeing our shores, chasing after foreign goods.

Because so many of our multinational firms operate without regard to the interests of the United States, a very distressing development can now be observed. While the share of the world's manufacturing undertaken in the United States has been declining since 1957, the amount of the world's manufacturing in the hands of U.S. multinationals has held steady or even increased. U.S. firms have been moving their manufacturing operations offshore to their overseas affiliates and have been closing American plants. In 1957, according to the figures from the National Bureau of Economic Research published in the January 18, 1987, *New York Times,* 22.7 percent of the world's manufacturing was carried out in the United States by U.S. multinationals and by companies operating only domestically; by 1983, the total was 13.9 percent. Yet during the same period, U.S. multinationals held on to a solid 17.7 percent of the world's manufacturing business, and actually increased their stakes in some categories but with less and less of that manufacturing undertaken domestically. The two figures taken together show that American multinationals and their investment strategies have had an enormously negative effect on our nation and have been responsible for systematically shifting high-paying jobs abroad.

Different countries have dealt with the third world in different ways. The conduct of our multinationals shows that we have generally perceived the third world as a vast pool of cheap labor to be used in the production of goods for markets both at home and abroad. Companies in other countries, especially in Japan, have not viewed the third world in those terms. Europeans, in particular, have been far more sophisticated; they have used inexpensive third world labor not to produce for their own home market, but to produce goods to be sold in the third world countries themselves. Although the German automobile and truck manufacturer Mercedes-Benz produces a full line of products in Brazil, it does not sell those products in Germany or in the rest of Europe. Brazilian-made Mercedes-Benz cars and trucks are sold in Latin America and Africa exclusively, posing no threat to the car company's European workers. Both Volvo and Volkswagen also follow similar strategies. These large, successful European multinationals have adopted strategies aimed at keeping their high-wage European workers employed producing for the high-priced European and American markets, while their low-wage workers in Latin America and elsewhere produce for the low-priced third world markets. They have preserved their domestic high-wage jobs and sacrificed nothing in profit or market share. In many instances,

Japanese multinationals have adopted these same approaches.

American multinationals, on the other hand, have been highly aggressive in bringing third world products to the home market without caring about the number of American jobs lost thereby. American car companies and electronics manufacturers have long been importing products built overseas for sale in our home market while ignoring the large markets within the third world itself. Recently, U.S. auto companies with operations in Korea that produce cars destined for America have even gone so far as to order parts from their competitors in Japan, rather than from their own factories in Detroit. These production agreements integrate Korean- and Japanese-made parts while excluding those made in America, even in the companies where the American partner is the dominant foreign participant.

One of the most successful new imports to reach our shores is Hyundai's Excel, which bears a striking resemblance to the Japanese imports of a few years back. In 1986, the first year Hyundais were available in the United States, 150,000 were sold, despite significant quality control problems. Although Hyundai's American dealers made a substantial profit from these cars, imports of Hyundais contributed heavily to the more than $5.1 billion trade deficit we had with Korea in 1986. Korea, which is a model NIC, still gladly receives foreign aid from us despite having such a favorable trade surplus.

A closer look reveals some interesting links between Hyundai and the Japanese. First, nearly 15 percent of Hyundai Motors is owned by the giant Japanese manufacturer Mitsubishi, which sells Hyundai many of the high-quality automotive parts used in the cars. Because of this arrangement, Korea, which has a massive trade surplus with us, maintains a large trade deficit with Japan—more than $4.2 billion. A great deal of the profits from Hyundai's sales in the United States thus ultimately go to Japan's Mitsubishi, the real power behind the success of the Hyundai car. But the Hyundai is not available in Japan, where it would compete with Japan's own manufacturers.

While the Japanese use the Koreans to launch a coordinated assault on the low end of the American automobile market, the American manufacturers use the Koreans to launch an attack on themselves. For instance, Pontiac's new Le Mans arrived in America in 1987 with first-year sales of about 170,000. The Le Mans is manufactured in Korea by Daewoo, which is 50 percent owned by General Motors, but receives technical assistance not from Detroit, but from GM's German affiliate, Adam Opel, as well as from its Japanese affiliate, Isuzu, and from its Japanese competitor Nissan. Americans were systematically left out of the Le Mans project, even though it was conceived by Pontiac for the United States— something the Japanese and Europeans would never do. Selling an offshore-produced Le Mans in the United States pits American workers against their low-wage Korean counterparts. Ultimately, as GM invests more heavily in Korea to produce for our home markets, there will be few high-wage U.S. workers left who can afford to buy new cars. But GM is not the only U.S. company that is pursuing what is ultimately a suicidal strategy.

Ford has just begun selling its Festiva line of cars that are produced in a joint venture between Ford, Kia Motors of Korea, and Japan's Mazda and C. Itoh. Dong-A, a manufacturer with links to Chrysler's new AMC division and to Toyota and Nissan as well, will soon be marketing trucks in the United States. And Samsung, one of Korea's biggest industrial concerns, has just agreed to make car parts for Chrysler.

In nearly every one of these ventures with third world Korea's fledgling, but already booming, auto industry, there is an American partner involved. What is truly astonishing is that in none of these arrangements is the Korean company using American-made or even American-designed parts; the parts that are not made in Korea are imported from Japan (more than 40 percent of the parts for the Ford Festiva are made by Mazda). In 1986 alone, the Japanese sold auto parts worth a total of $400 million to Korean manufacturers and provided millions more dollars' worth of design and engineering services. In the same year, American companies sold next to nothing to their Korean affiliates.

Arrangements such as these raise some very serious concerns about the more than dubious deal-making prowess of our multinationals, and raise as well questions about whether these companies, unlike their European and Japanese counterparts, have any concern for the impact their actions will have on the future of our nation.

As an increasing number of our multinationals institutionalize this kind of trade, the balance-of-payments deficits cannot help but grow. That is one reason for the increase in the trade deficit figures for 1987 despite the large devaluations of the dollar. Companies are simply unable to shift to domestic suppliers while the number, variety, and type of U.S. goods for export have dwindled.

What is worse is that the development of intracompany trade with the third world is rapidly becoming a precondition for being able to compete in the U.S. market as companies accustom themselves to third world wage scales. The lure of $1 per hour wages, as opposed to domestic wages of more than $10 per hour, encourages producers to shift investment offshore rather than to make a commitment to the nation's future by investing in highly automated domestic factories and better management. For a large multinational company run by accountants interested more in profit and risk avoidance than in our country's survival, the short-term certainty of producing at low cost in Taiwan, even with dire consequences for our balance of payments, is preferable to the longer term strategy of keeping production at home. Even our new exports of services, such as state-of-the-art computer software and insurance and banking services, which are not immune to foreign competition, fail miserably to offset imports of as many as 2 to 3 million foreign-made cars per year (many made by the affiliates of U.S. manufacturers) or 3 to 4 million VCRs, or, most tragically, tons of agricultural products grown in Mexico and as far away as Argentina, while our farmers go broke.

The debacle of American investment in the third world, and the way it turned against us, began only in this century.

Investment in the third world started slowly. In the first phase, plants were located overseas to be close to a certain raw material source. For example, Firestone Tire and Rubber originally set up operations in Malaysia to be close to the rubber trees and plantations. Much of this kind of investment occurred during the early part of the century through the 1920s when the United States was first becoming an international economic power.

The second phase enabled American companies to export to those countries. Offices of American firms set up to promote our exports were commonplace during the 1920s and 1930s as the United States became more powerful globally, producing products known for their utility, quality, durability, and simplicity of design—attributes that now describe Japanese goods. American products, whether outboard engines or tractors, were thought to be especially well suited to the tough conditions of the developing world and that is when names like Ford Motor, Caterpillar Tractor, Evenrude Outboard, Mack Truck, Douglas Aircraft, General Electric, RCA, and a host of others became internationally renowned symbols of state-of-the-art manufacturing and design. Americans could travel to the farthest reaches of the globe confident that they would find their products well used and highly regarded and, as a result, their country respected as the great engine of industrial might and innovation.

The third phase of American investment in the South began when American industrialists opened plants overseas primarily in the larger developing countries, owing to increased competition within the third world between American and European producers. Building Ford cars in Brazil meant that they could be sold at prices reflecting Brazilian wage rates and without the added cost of shipping. Finished parts in the form of kits could be sent from Detroit for assembly in Brazil (later the entire car would be produced there) at prices much more favorable to the Brazilian market than the cars produced in Europe or Detroit. Locating American plants in these countries greatly increased our influence while also upgrading the skills of the foreign workers. Locating plants in these countries also enabled us to sell to other developing countries in the same geographic region or even in other regions, so General Motors Brazil could export its trucks to the Middle East and General Electric of Malaysia could export to the Philippines. R. Buckminster Fuller, the brilliant engineer, mathematician, and designer, said that during the 1950s America's greatest export was its factories, since we built plants in nearly every developing, and developed, country of the world. Many of those factories were more advanced than their counterparts in the United States. India, Brazil, Nigeria, Korea, Taiwan, Malaysia, Singapore, Thailand, and Mexico were just a few of the countries to receive massive levels of U.S. investment. Japan is now building factories around the world at a furious pace, as we once did. But there is no evidence as yet that Japanese companies are importing cheap parts from overseas plants to be used in the products they sell in their home market, although Honda recently said it may begin selling some U.S.-made cars in Japan. Whether this is a serious gesture or mere public relations will only be determined when we know how many U.S.-built cars make it to Japan.

Had America stopped at phase three, selling products produced in the third world exclusively in third world markets, we would probably have continued to be a very prosperous, high-wage manufacturing country. In all probability, we also would have been in a far better position to avoid the Decline and Crash of the economy. At the same time, producing products in and for the third world would have benefited the consumers in those regions and helped transfer needed skills to developing countries. Most important for us, however, is the fact that had we continued to sell in the third world from plants located there, profits from those operations would eventually have reached our shores with net positive results when figured into our trade statistics. Had we continued in this phase, just about the worst consequence of our relationship would have been that some countries might have pressured our companies to take in local partners, with few serious consequences. Also, without a doubt, other countries, developed and developing, would certainly have begun to compete with us in these markets, but we would have been deeply entrenched in these countries and our home markets would have been safe, with high-wage U.S. workers producing for the home market as well as for other high-priced markets abroad.

The problem began when U.S. firms started to sell the products they manufactured abroad in our home market. This kind of self-inflicted competition has been extremely damaging to our long-term success. The consumer electronics industry was the first casualty when, in the middle 1960s, GE and RCA began importing foreign-made radios and televisions in an all-out effort to shave costs and gain market share. What did this mean to the consumer? At first, very little, since the imported brands marketed through the large American multinationals were not priced much lower than domestic-made products. But to the shareholders, imported goods meant higher profits.

During this fourth phase of investment in the third world, the emphasis of American business suddenly shifted from the long term to the short term as very rapidly a plethora of low-cost, usually low-quality imported goods became available that could be easily substituted for the (then) higher quality, more expensive, domestically manufactured products. American investment in the third world suddenly skyrocketed to more than $53 billion, as of 1984, as corporate money managers realized they could slash expenses by getting out of domestic manufacturing. During this phase in our relations with the third world our trade figures began to sink into the red, as we began to manufacture less and import more from everyone. For example, since 1981 alone, our exports to Latin America declined by more than $23.4 billion—not just because of their debt problems, but also because we have less to sell them compared with the Europeans and Japanese.

If taken as an isolated phenomenon, one obvious solution to our growing balance-of-payments deficit with the third world would be to impose tariffs on imports from those countries, like Brazil, Korea, or Taiwan, with whom we have large negative balances. But because of the close links between different operating divisions of our own multinational corporations, according to the Overseas Development Council (*Policy Focus,* No. 7, 1985), the imposition of high tariffs on these countries "would also reduce the profitability of U.S. affiliates overseas," ultimately reducing the profits of the domestic parent companies as well. Even with recession running rampant in the third world, as of 1987 American companies overseas produced about $13 billion in earnings for their domestic affiliates from their sales in third world markets, according to the Department of Commerce. Without that income, our balance-of-payments woes would have been worse. What those figures conceal, though, is the lost income of the American worker whose company has ceased to export.

As a result of the rapid increase in imports from the third world, many of our businesses have become inextricably linked to the fortunes of the developing countries. It is now not so strange to consider that even when the countries of the third world and the United States were clearly at loggerheads over politics and policy at the United Nations, the fact of economic interdependence was recognized. Moreover, even during the most protracted and bitter negotiations (outside of OPEC), the third world never sought to destroy the economy of the United States. Third world leaders generally recognize that prosperity in the United States is vital to prosperity in their own lands, and that, more and more, the reverse is true.

The third world—economically so much weaker than Europe or Japan—has moved next door to the United States through the multinational corporation. Yet in spite of the links between the United States and the third world, we have failed to delineate a strategy that is truly in the best interests of both. As long as we ignore the importance of the third world, we do so at the risk of our own future prosperity. We should do what the Japanese are doing—study the economies of the third world in minute detail, and then formulate plans to prosper from our relationships with these countries.

The Japanese Ministry for International Trade and Industry (MITI) even has a special research branch, the Institute for Developing Economies, charged with finding ways to enhance Japanese exports and investment in third world countries. If we fail to do this, when the third world reemerges from its recession we will have missed making it a market for our goods, and we will come face-to-face with a powerful competitor in large measure financed and even trained by our own "loyal" multinational corporations.

7

GLOBAL COMPETITION AND THE INVESTMENT GAP

BOEING is the nation's largest exporting company with orders on its books for planes worth more than $16 billion. But airplanes are nowhere near our biggest export, nor are computers nor even wheat. Thanks to the Decline and Crash of the economy, our biggest exports are financial. Foreigners are buying more American debt, in the form of corporate and governmental notes and bonds, than ever before. They are also buying up equity in the form of stocks and real estate and using the profits they derive from these purchases to boost their wealth to new heights.

While outright takeovers usually make the business pages of the newspaper, quiet buying goes unnoticed except for its effect on the price of a stock. The sale of corporate and governmental debt to foreigners also makes no news, but to support the sale of that dreaded debt interest rates must remain sky high. The impact of these large debt offerings will be observed in future decreases in our standard of living coupled with a further loss of control over our economic destiny.

Foreign money is rushing into this country to buy our debt and purchase stocks and other assets at an incredible rate. In 1986 alone foreigners purchased $127 billion worth of American assets, while we sold them back $32 billion of our foreign holdings; 1987 foreign purchases are even higher. To give an example of the magnitude of these purchases, America's sale of assets in 1986 alone was $21 billion greater than all of Brazil's foreign debt combined. We worry about the consequences of Brazil's foreign debt, which was built up over a twenty-year period, but we have hardly given a thought to the even larger transfers of our assets occurring every year. By our standards, debt-plagued Brazil is a piker.

Total investment by foreigners in the United States is now up to $1.2 trillion, more than double what it was in 1981 and more than one-quarter of our total GNP, with most of it invested in financial assets, such as stocks, bonds, and government debt. Foreign ownership of America is now nearly half the size of our total federal debt with the greatest gains having been made by foreigners during the Reagan years.

Even the tremendous run-up of stocks in 1985–1987, as the Dow surged past the 2700 mark, was largely fueled by foreign money racing into the United States. Forty billion dollars in foreign stock purchases alone are expected by the end of 1987. Years of mismanagement dating back to the Vietnam War have flooded Europe and Japan with dollars, and now those dollars are buying our stocks and contributing to their volatility.

The more recent trade gaps that have developed during the Reagan years have also served to fill our trading partners' bank accounts with enough cash to buy out America. In 1986 the Japanese had a trade surplus of nearly $60 billion, triple their 1982 level, and in 1987, even with the dollar's 40 percent fall in value against the yen, the trade gap is expected to increase, to a total with all countries of at least $159 billion. Our trading picture with Germany alone has gone from positive, before Reagan assumed office, to nearly

$20 billion in the red in 1986. With such a loss of dollars owing to our inability to produce goods for export, it is no wonder that our assets are making their way overseas while foreigners take advantage of our high interest rates.

The internationalization of American debt, the erosion of our position in world trade, and the transition of our country from manufacturer to importer mean it is extremely unlikely we will ever again be able to act as freely as we once did economically. We may never again have a free enough hand to stimulate the kind of investment we need to become competitive once more. The reason our investments will be slim in the future is that we must keep our interest rates high enough to convince foreigners to loan us money. High rates may be able to pull in enough money to fund our nation's annual budget deficit, but they powerfully discourage longer term productive investment. If foreign money managers stopped investing in the United States altogether, our interest rates would have to climb much higher to raise enough money to fund our debt.

As long as we can promise high interest rates we need not fear that our foreign creditors will cease financing the federal government's spending spree. That has been the way we have sold our debt overseas since the advent of the Reagan administration with its insistence on cutting taxes while raising defense outlays. But high interest rates cut into profits, raise the cost of doing business, and discourage new investment by our own companies. High interest rates also set the overall climate for other types of investment. For example, if an investor in the bond market can make a 10 percent return on his investment from buying IBM triple-A bonds, he will require at least that rate of return from his other investments as well. This forces companies to pay their stockholders greater dividend earnings, at the expense of new investment, and deters them from embarking upon longer range projects that require research. A high interest rate environment pervades every investment decision because it sets a certain minimum rate of return an investor can get for doing nothing more than parking his money in a bond, Treasury note, or bank. And because we must continually seek new sources of capital to fund our growing federal debt (since no politician seems bold enough to either raise taxes or cut spending), the high interest rate climate can only persist. As long as high rates exist, they will do great damage to our most productive and research-sensitive sectors of the economy. But the urgent need to finance our debt has also hampered the Federal Reserve's ability to stimulate growth, during a recession, or to restrain growth, to fight inflation. High interest rates have tied the hands of policymakers and removed important items from the nation's economic tool chest.

In the past, the Fed could stimulate the economy by creating more money and/or by cutting various interest rates to make cheaper money available for consumption or investment purposes. Today, if the Fed lowers its interest rates, we run the risk of losing foreign investors who are at present purchasing our debt. The delicacy of the Fed's predicament with respect to interest rates was recently summed up very succinctly by the editors of the January 1987 *Dun's Business Month:* "If little capital moves abroad, lower interest rates will powerfully stimulate the U.S. economy. If, on the other hand, lower rates trigger a massive flight from the dollar, higher import prices will inject a strong dose of inflation into the economy, which would discourage the very business spending the Fed wanted to stimulate." In other words, because we have elected a government that believes it is better to borrow from abroad than tax at home, we have lost much of our control over interest rates, inflation, and the value of the dollar.

Because the Fed must now take into account not only the domestic consequences of its actions but foreign reactions as well, it has made the job of its Board of Governors impossibly hard. Not only must they be able to forecast how Wall Street will react to their policies, they must also guess how financial managers in Bonn, London, Paris, and Tokyo will regard what they do. While the Fed tries to figure out how our foreign creditors will react to their decisions, Congress and the president show no concern with the consequences of their own policy actions. As a result they have had the dubious distinction of promulgating two or more highly contradictory policies at the same time.

For example, in 1981, against a backdrop of increased defense spending, the first of the Reagan tax cuts went into effect. As a result of the sudden increase in the federal deficit occasioned by greater spending and less revenue, interest crept upward because of all the extra borrowing by the government to fund that debt. Foreign investors eager to take advantage of our rising rates exchanged their currencies for dollars to buy our bonds and notes; these purchases of dollars drove its value skyward. As the dollar's value soared the prices of imported goods like cars, cameras, and VCRs decreased rapidly. Consumers flush with cash as a result of the tax cut began buying these imported goods in record volume, which, for the first time, pushed our own trade in manufactured goods into the red. What was the final outcome of such a contradictory policy? Far from stimulating our economy, the tax cut stimulated the economies of Europe and Japan.

As more foreign funds flooded into our country to buy the government's high-quality, high-interest-rate notes, the value of the dollar was driven up even further. A rate of exchange of $1.84 to the British pound has been in effect since 1987, but in 1984 it was at near parity. When the dollar was so expensive, our manufacturing firms lost their international competitiveness. As a result, the trade deficit grew greater as our exports slumped and American firms moved more of their factories offshore and increased their imports.

This policy fiasco was happening about the same time that President Reagan gave former interior secretary James Watt the dubious award of a foot with a bullet hole shot in it for Watt's candid but less than brilliant remarks (Watt said that he thought offshore oil platforms enhanced the beauty of the rugged California coast). It seems Reagan's economic advisers could have qualified for the award just as well since the culmination of the 1981 tax cut could be seen in the 1982 recession, which affected not only our country but half the world as well.

Recovery from the 1982 recession has been partial at best. Official unemployment figures may hover at about or just below 6 percent, but there are great numbers of discouraged workers who no longer are counted among the unemployed, several hundred thousand part-time workers who wish to work longer hours, with nearly two and a half million jobs in the manufacturing sector lost.

Although we have since at least partly awakened from the curse of voodoo economics, other countries have not. Among the remaining sufferers are the debtor countries of the third world with their billions in variable-interest-rate loans. As our interest rates went up, their payments followed suit, forcing them to cut back their purchases of our goods and curtail their development plans. These countries, most of which are still crippled from the run-up in their overall debt and the rise in our interest rates, have historically been the second largest purchasers of our exports. In one bold tax and spending policy move during 1981 we brought our economy to a halt while simultaneously destroying the second largest export market for our goods.

The government has lost other policy options as a result of our tremendous level of indebtedness to foreign creditors. For example, a policy of stimulating the economy through fiscal measures is based on the ability of Congress to either cut taxes or increase spending; a policy of stimulating the economy through monetary measures stems from our ability to increase the money supply or make money cheaper to borrow. From an economic standpoint both measures are supposed to put more money into the hands of corporations and individuals to enable them to buy more, invest more, and produce more. People are buying more—imported goods and with credit—and the investment levels of American companies are low and falling further. Yet, strange as it may seem, even with a falling rate of investment, Congress and the president saw fit to remove some very significant tax incentives for capital investment from the Tax Reform Act of 1987.

Traditionally we have applied a mix of fiscal and monetary policies to manage the economy and keep it on a more or less even keel. During times of recession the monetary policy of the Fed has been to open up the money spigot while the fiscal policy of the Congress has been to boost spending or cut taxes. Together these measures worked fairly well until the mid-1970s, keeping investment at levels that were respectable but not exemplary.

In normal times fiscal and monetary policies can stimulate investment, but these policies cannot be put into full force during these Decline and Crash times. This loss of control over our economy will keep us from investing the necessary funds to become competitive once again. Without these funds our standard of living will slip behind those countries that we aided after World War II as our rate of productivity lags. Without immediate reforms to stimulate investment we will have no way to reassert our economic leadership.

OUR investment requirements are very large if we are to become competitive as an industrial country. For example, as early as 1981, before the full force of the Reagan presidency lulled the country into a false sense of security about the future, the Council of State Planning Agencies, at the behest of the nation's governors, looked at the condition of our national infrastructure, our roads, bridges, railroads, electric power grids, ports, water resources, etc., and issued its landmark report titled "America in Ruins." Not long after the topic of a deteriorating America made news there was intense discussion about how much all this needed investment will cost. Estimates vary, but range between $2 trillion and $3 trillion for infrastructure repair with another $2 trillion needed to fully modernize industry—both astronomical sums equal to twice the amount so far spent on the Reagan arms buildup. This combined figure of about $4.5 trillion over about a ten-year period works out to about $18,000 per

American, and it is enough to put us on top, once again, with a world-class industry operating under world-class conditions. It is also enough to end our Decline and Crash. But where will these sums come from, and how will we raise it?

Congress has traditionally used its fiscal policy measures to pay for new public investment and stimulate new private investment. Tax credits, or reductions, can be written into laws that would make it worthwhile for American companies to invest here instead of abroad. New taxes, temporary increases in the federal deficit, and moving funds from one program to another are the traditional ways to deal with needed investment in the infrastructure. If the tax incentives are able to spur businesses to invest and become competitive once again, then little will need to be done to limit imports. The excellence of our industry will be enough to keep the balance-of-payments picture in the black. But so far Congress has done little else than limit imports in the vain hope that this will enhance our competitiveness.

Consider how precarious our situation has become. With about $200 billion more owed to foreigners than they owe to us, nearly 10 percent of our total national debt, and another $200 billion that must be paid out annually from taxes to service our debt, the government has a huge requirement for new funds even without any redevelopment of our industry or infrastructure. Interest rates have been high to keep funds flowing into the United States to finance that debt.

Raising additional money for new investment in public infrastructure means tax hikes or further borrowing, and if industry is also prodded to make its needed investments the level of borrowing will climb even higher. Government and business going into the world's financing markets at the same time for their respective modernizations will create mountains of new debt and force us to increase the flow of funds from abroad. But what if other governments object? As early as 1981 Germany's chancellor Helmut Schmidt protested America's policy of borrowing from Europe rather than raising taxes at home because he felt that our borrowing was so massive and at such high interest rates that it was diverting funds from German investment as well as driving up interest rates around the world. Schmidt's position, which was echoed by other European leaders, is likely to reemerge if an American investment offensive is launched.

To pay for needed public investment, Congress's simplest fiscal policy option is to raise taxes over a ten-year period to pay for the $3 trillion in new infrastructure development. But annual tax hikes of $300 billion per year will take significantly more money out of consumers' hands and put a severe damper on spending and saving. Tax hikes of such magnitude will be politically unpopular, and will also make the United States far less attractive to foreign investors. While it's true that the money spent on infrastructure maintenance and rebuilding will eventually serve as a stimulus to the economy as workers spend their wages, it will take time for the effect to produce significant results.

The second fiscal policy option is for Congress to defer paying for the $3 trillion modernization by adding it to the national debt and financing it through more borrowing. But this means that an extra $300 billion in loans must be sold to foreigners each year. Making an additional $300 billion per year in new debt attractive means raising interest rates sufficiently above those in other countries to attract their funds. However, American firms would also pay those same higher rates to borrow what they need for their own modernization programs. Moreover, raising American rates above those of the rest of the world means that foreigners will rush to the dollar and thus drive up its price. A high dollar means American firms won't be able to export, which cancels out much of the incentive for investment in new industrial plants. So as borrowing from abroad increases, the value of the dollar increases which increases the cost of doing business in a way that cancels out most of the incentives for investment.

But suppose Congress opts for first making it more attractive for companies to invest the $1.9 trillion needed to gain competitiveness by cutting taxes before it invests in the upgrading of our infrastructure? In such a scenario the government again comes up against its own limitations because if taxes are cut without equal spending curtailments then the size of the federal deficit will increase. If the deficit goes up, it will carry interest rates up with it and the value of the dollar will once again soar as foreigners rush to loan us money. Once more the effect of the incentive will be lost as interest rates increase the cost of investment and a high dollar causes exports to suffer.

In the current climate, there are no options but reducing taxes and expenditures at the same time if interest rates are to be allowed to return to levels where they do not deter investment. So far this bit of common sense has escaped even the best brains of the Reagan administration. Just consider that the supply-side theorists in Washington somehow were able to recommend that taxes be shaved as spending was increased drastically. In 1979, at the end of the Carter administration, outlays for the military amounted to $116.3 billion; in 1987, despite the 1981 and 1987 tax cuts, military outlays had increased to more than $282.2 billion. Total governmental outlays also grew from $463.3 billion in 1979 to $831.2 billion in 1987, an increase of nearly 45 percent, while taxes were cut to the bone.

If the world were perfect and Congress were allowed to apply its fiscal tax relief medicine to foster the needed $1.9 trillion investment in America's ailing industry without increasing its borrowing, it would have to do so by making real cuts in the budget, as already mentioned. But real cuts, as Lester Thurow pointed out in *The Zero Sum Society*, are political. If Congress sticks to its principles and refuses to borrow, decisions will have to be made about which programs to cut and which to save. If Congress is ill equipped to make these choices, other strategies must be sought to regain control over our economy. What strategies must we follow? Those that promote rapid growth. And paramount among them are those that unlock new markets for our goods.

Even with rapid growth the size of the needed investment is still massive. Perhaps these gigantic amounts can be extended over a twenty-year period, but even so they would still impose a burden, and they would have to fight with other pet projects of the government, such as Star Wars, with its own $1 trillion to $2 trillion price tag. Star Wars will not return any benefit to the economy unless there is a nuclear war and the Star Wars defensive shield actually works. But the investment in our infrastructure and industry will have immediate results. To redevelop our nation we must first redevelop our markets in the debt-plagued third world.

8

FULL SPEED IN THE WRONG DIRECTION

BACK in the early 1970s, at the height of American prosperity and power, a small group of primarily European intellectuals were brought together by a dashing Italian businessman, Aurelio Peccei, a former managing director of Olivetti, to discuss what they felt were the critical problems facing humanity. The group, which came to be known as the Club of Rome, because their first meeting took place near Peccei's home in the Eternal City, saw a future of declining possibilities for humanity. The findings of the Club of Rome ultimately would not only contribute to the Decline and Crash of our economy, but would also sow seeds of deep confusion and disarray among our allies and trading partners and add to our conflicts with the third world.

This group of 100 intellectuals and business leaders from around the world was especially interested in the planet's oil and raw material resources and concerned about growing scarcities of these products. Together the members hired two American computer modelers, a husband and wife team from

Dartmouth University, Dennis and Donella Meadows, to build a computer model that would mimic the world's usage of primary products and help in forecasting future availability. The Meadowses had been trained at M.I.T. under James Forrester, a gifted pioneer in the use of computers to simulate economic processes and a noted pessimist about the future. Much of the Meadowses' work was based on Forrester's gloomy assumptions about the future supply of raw materials and other commodities.

When the model was completed in 1972, the Club of Rome issued its now famous book *The Limits to Growth* (New York: Potomac Assoc., 1972), amidst a tremendous barrage of global publicity. So startling were the Meadowses' projections that the world was stunned; the Meadowses asserted that at the then-present levels of usage, no matter what happened, world industrial production would be hobbled by growing and irreversible scarcities of energy and primary products. The basic stocks of vital raw materials in the world would be depleted, in some cases as early as the year 2000, and as this unavoidable depletion of resources took place, pollution levels would rise alarmingly and industrial society would be forced to contract drastically. The Club of Rome asserted that we were entering a period of deep resource scarcities and even, according to some members, "mega-famines."

Why should we discuss the Club of Rome in the context of America's current Decline and Crash? Because the biased and incorrect assumptions contained in *The Limits to Growth* have colored the way we view the future and have given leaders worldwide a set of highly erroneous assumptions. In that one slim volume, the Club of Rome overturned the long-standing post–World War II ideal of a world growing together through mutual trade and replaced it with the idea that one country's wealth can be gained at the expense of another's.

After the Club's initial report, many people in government here and abroad were persuaded by the thesis. For some reason, the notion that we were doomed to a future of increasing scarcities, eventual famines, and heavy pollution, which no human actions could counter, struck a responsive chord—and people embraced this set of assumptions almost religiously. The 1974 Arab oil embargo of the United States, with its halted shipments of crude oil and long gas lines at the pump, occurred just after the publication of this first Club of Rome book and seemed an ominous portent of things to come. No matter that the oil embargo was a manufactured political act rather than the first sign of coming energy scarcities. With the groundwork laid by the Club, the oil embargo was enough to convince many jittery people that we were running out of almost everything. In a strange way, during the decade of the 1970s, economic growth came to be seen as an enemy. The influence of this point of view was pervasive.

The trouble with the Club of Rome's report was not just that it was pessimistic about the future. Had enough concerned and influential people shared that sense of pessimism in the early 1970s, they might have taken actions that would have forestalled our Decline and Crash. Instead, the Club of Rome did a colossal disservice to humanity by naively shifting the focus of the debate on the future from economics, management, politics, technology, and business—human constructs over which we have some measure of control—to the amount of resources left in the ground. While shifting our attention from issues of management to the quantities of various natural products, the Club ignored the fact that, in most cases, plentiful substitutes exist for each product they labeled as scarce. From my own experience, working with teams of researchers around the world and at the United Nations, I saw that acceptance of the Club's model went virtually unquestioned and unchallenged.

This shift in emphasis from something we can control to something we cannot control convinced many people, and among them many of the world's leaders, that the growth of one country could only be achieved at the expense of another. While it is true that the United States in particular and the world in general have never operated at peak levels of efficiency with respect to resources, energy, and even manpower, the Club's report dismissed any notions that future resource catastrophies could be averted by developing our capacity to "do more with less."

The Club of Rome study can be likened to a well-intentioned naval architect of the 1820s predicting the rapid deforestation of the planet owing to the great increase in world trade. After all, his logic might say, world trade is now growing faster than ever before, which means that each year more ships will have to be built. And since ships are made of wood, trees will have to be cut down so that by the end of the century no forests would be left.

The problem with the naval architect's view is easy for us to recognize. Not only can forests be replanted but within a few years technology would advance to the point where nearly all ships would be made of steel. Instead of confronting a shortage of wood for ships, the world would turn to other raw materials.

Yet in spite of its misplaced emphasis, several countries were influenced by this study and its insistence on the paramount importance of raw material endowments over technology and the ability to recycle and reduce pollution through abatement programs. The Swedish government established a center to study the future and one of its first books was entitled *How Much Is Enough?* which called for a future of limited growth and a return to simpler values. Other studies issued from groups calling for "no-growth" sustainable societies. There was also the movement toward "voluntary simplicity" in light of the Club's grim projections. And some groups linked the Club's findings to the conservation and ecological movements.

Under the Club of Rome's sway, in the mid-1970s, iconoclastic Texas oil, gas and real estate millionaire George Mitchell began giving out a biannual $50,000 prize and hosting huge conferences (several of which I attended) with academics invited from all over the world to search for what he called "alternatives to growth." And in California, Jerry Brown was swept into office as governor on a political platform proclaiming that America had entered the "era of limits."

Even Canada, despite being the world's second most richly endowed country, was overcome with Club of Rome fever and issued its own gloomy *Canada* 2000 report while the prime minister at the time, Pierre Trudeau, a friend of Aurelio Peccei's, played host to meetings of the Club's members. Mexico, too, was influenced by the Club of Rome; Luis Echeverría, the former president of Mexico, even wrote a book with Peccei on world events. In the United States, President Carter, also under the sway of the Club's apocalyptic vision, commissioned his own study, called *Global* 2000, which, true to form, predicted widespread global resource calamities. Of all the advanced, industrial countries, Japan alone seemed unswayed by the arguments of the Club of Rome even though Saburo Okita, one of Japan's foremost economists and one of the architects of its phenomenal growth, supported the Club's efforts to survey the future and conduct its first study.

While so many in the developed world embraced the Club of Rome's concept of a future made difficult and harsh by growing scarcities of energy and raw materials, the developing countries were not so convinced. In fact, many scholars in third world countries saw the Club of Rome as a highly malevolent force sapping the economic vitality of the developed world by advocating a retreat from growth. What's more, to those specialists, whose vision of events was often more concrete than that of the academics of the Club of Rome, the West's lack of criticism of the Club's report reflected not so much an acceptance of the underlying assumptions as a nagging sense of guilt for having become rich. As one Korean diplomat told me during a meeting of American and European economists in Seoul just about the time of Jimmy Carter's 1979 speech on America's moral decadence, "If you people in the West are unhappy with your wealth, and fear running out of resources, then give them up. But we in the third world have not yet grown so rich that we can afford the luxury of complaining that we have too much."

With this kind of hard-headed analysis, Korea managed to keep a positive trade balance with the OPEC countries in spite of the run-up in the price of oil (something we could never do even with our enviable deposits of oil in Texas, California, Oklahoma, and Alaska) and grow at enviable rates even during the worst of the Reagan recession of the early 1980s. During the decade of the 1970s when all the world was cautioned not to grow, Korea, skeptical of the doomsayers and perceptive enough to realize that the content of the Club of Rome report reflected more a philosophical than an objective interpretation of the facts, was able to propel itself from the ranks of the backward countries into the league of medium-developed countries.

In spite of those few pockets of enlightenment in policy-making circles around the world, the developing world was as much hypnotized as was the West into believing that the major obstacle to a future of worldwide wealth was the supposed scarcity of raw materials and energy. Such voices in the wilderness as R. Buckminster Fuller, who convincingly demonstrated that we had achieved ever greater efficiencies of raw material use, and the defense strategist and planner Herman Kahn, who showed that the Club of Rome's computer model of resource use was faulty at best, were ignored by the institutionalized pessimists in our government.

Because we accepted the Club of Rome's vision and Japan did not, we busied ourselves creating stockpiles of so-called vital resources, which tied up billions of dollars' worth of investment capital, while Japan went the other way, converting itself into a "just-in-time" society maintaining only the most minute quantities of vital products. Our stockpiling of resources is all the more ludicrous if we consider that North America, from Mexico to Canada, contains many of the earth's richest deposits of nearly every vital resource, including oil, coal, gold, and nearly every other metal, as well as huge surpluses of nearly every type of agricultural product, while Japan is resource bare. Our analysis of the future made us invest in commodities in spite of our resources; Japan's analysis prodded it to invest in machines, education, training, and research in the belief that the human factor is by far the most important component of a nation's wealth.

Most hurt by the predictions of the Club of Rome were

the energy and commodity producers themselves. During the 1970s the prices of raw materials everywhere soared as a result of the mismanagement of the dollar, the sudden onset of global inflation, speculation about impending scarcities, increases in global demand, and the new power of cartels like OPEC. For example, in real terms, according to the 1970–1985 United Nations' monthly *Bulletin of Statistics* and the U.N. Conference on Trade and Development's monthly *Commodity Price Bulletin,* world prices for food commodities more than doubled between 1970 and 1975, as did the price of all minerals, while the combined average prices for *all* commodities priced in dollars (excluding oil) rose by more than 100 percent between 1970 and 1980. During that same decade, the price of oil showed a more than eightfold increase. None of these price increases, though, was due to real shortages or even to decreased supply but to bad management of the dollar and to the expectation of future shortages.

Fueled by the prognostications of massive scarcities, the owners of commodity-producing mines, farms, and plantations viewed their investments in inflated terms. The prices of farmland in Kansas, Montana, and Argentina were swept to new highs, as were the prices of bauxite mines in Jamaica and Guayana and oil fields in California, Alaska, and Indonesia. Buoyed by the rapidly rising prices, commodity producers borrowed heavily from the banks. Oil field equipment producers and oil companies were so flush with capital from the drilling boom that they began acquiring companies in areas that were supposed to survive the coming resource scarcities. Exxon started a high-tech office machine company, which later went bust, and Schlumberger acquired Fairchild, the large producer of semiconductors, and promptly ran it into the ground. But with plentiful and even growing supplies of raw materials, the commodity highs of the 1970s soon turned into a bust during the 1980s, with rapidly falling prices.

Even with all of OPEC's billions, and in spite of a special research fund set up by the OPEC members in Vienna (headed by a Club of Rome supporter), the oil cartel smugly ignored one of the most basic tenets of economics: If the prices for a good, service, or commodity rise high enough, people will soon find cheaper substitutes. Only very late in the game did Saudi Arabia's former oil minister Sheik Yamani wake up to the fact that expensive oil was starting to mobilize the industrialized countries into finding alternatives—alternatives that in many cases had been developed decades earlier during World War II as substitutes for products made scarce by the fighting. With the price of oil climbing, Brazil was even able to mandate a shift from gas-fueled cars to cars powered by alcohol. Mixtures of gas and alcohol were even beginning to show up in the United States and in Europe.

During the 1970s the magic threshold price for oil (that is, the price at which consumers began seriously to seek alternatives to traditional oil sources) was about $27 per barrel. When the price of oil rose to that level a number of alternative sources suddenly seemed attractive. For instance, at $27 per barrel, "stripper" wells in the United States (those tens of thousands of small wells that produce fewer than 10 barrels a day) became profitable. At $27 per barrel North Sea oil and oil from Alaska's Prudhoe Bay could be easily lifted and sold at a profit, and countries and companies could afford the massive investment needed in offshore platforms, pipelines through frozen tundra, and new, fast Japanese supertankers. At that price, it became profitable to invest in technologies that could exploit even the lower grade oil shale and tar sands in Canada and the waxy, heavy crude deposits in Venezuela. When the price hit $27 per barrel the Gulf of Mexico could be explored, as could vast areas of the western part of the United States. In other words, the first consequence of the price of oil rising above threshold was that both the supply of oil and the number of suppliers increased, with the biggest increases seen among non-OPEC producers. Rather than oil shortages, by the early 1980s one of the world's biggest problems was the sudden glut.

With the price of oil beginning to falter in 1983, proposals were floated, but rejected, to tax foreign oil by $5 or $10 per barrel. Taxing foreign oil would have done a great deal to increase domestic supply, cut imports, shrink the balance-of-payments deficit, and provide added revenue to the government with no significant impact on the price of gas at the pump. More important, a tax that would keep OPEC's oil priced higher than our own would have helped break the oil cartel and loosen its stranglehold on the world. Even though this rather sane and painless proposal would have helped eradicate the national debt, it was never implemented owing to opposition by the White House and the oil interests.

Even as new sources of oil became available, so that an excess of supply and a price collapse were both imminent, our banks continued to lend billions of dollars to oil-producing countries such as Mexico, Venezuela, Nigeria, and Indonesia and to fund big investments in the "oil patch" in our own country—so widespread was the Club of Rome's idea of impending resources scarcities.

As the prices of oil and other commodities rose, conservation increased while consumption decreased—just as classical economics predicted it should. According to oil expert S. Fred Singer, a geophysicist and professor of environmental science at the University of Virginia (writing in the *Resourceful Earth*, edited by Julian Simon and Herman Kahn; New York: Blackwell, 1984), global demand for oil decreased from a peak of about 62 million barrels per day in 1979 to about 58 million barrels per day in 1984—a loss in demand greater than the average daily output of Saudi Arabia. At the same time, because of the rapid price rises for oil, the world became much more efficient in its use of energy with each successive "oil price shock" giving rise to subsequent increases in worldwide efficiency of use.

OPEC chose to ignore the growing efficiencies, the new sources of non-OPEC oil, and the other sources of energy coming onstream, foreshadowed by the beginnings of President Carter's synthetic oils program. All of those signs were readily observable, but OPEC in its greed and dogged belief in a coming supply scarcity continued driving prices upward. As prices began to inch toward the $40 per barrel peak, supplies grew so quickly that, despite the embargo on Libyan crude resulting from its sponsorship of terrorism, and Iran and Iraq warring and producing far below their capacities, there was an oil glut. Even with President Reagan's intervention into the market by canceling the Carter synthetic oil program and buying massive amounts of oil on the world market to fill the salt domes of our so-called strategic oil stockpile, the high price of oil could not be maintained. Within an eighteen-month period, from early 1985 to mid-1987, the price of oil plummeted from the high $30s to just above $10 per barrel before climbing back somewhat. If these dollar figures are corrected for inflation, they show that oil producers today are actually receiving less for their oil than they did in the early 1950s. Yet, owing to decades of borrowing, their debt levels are hundreds of times larger than they were during the 1950s, a fact which puts our banks in jeopardy and causes these commodity-exporting nations to curtail their imports of American-made goods and services.

The world is weaker because the price of oil fell. Mexico and Nigeria, two of our biggest suppliers, are hopelessly in debt to our banks, and with oil prices low and oil export revenues falling they will never be able to repay that debt. Ecuador and Venezuela are also teetering on the edge of insolvency because of the oil glut. Nigeria is also deeply in trouble; many of its biggest development projects have been curtailed.

Even Saudi Arabia, while not exactly poor, is feeling the pinch. The 1987 budget figures for that giant OPEC producer—released after a significant delay of nine and a half months—are both illustrative and alarming: Government oil revenue has plunged from a high in 1982 of $100 billion to less than $20 billion in 1987; gross domestic product has slumped from nearly $160 billion in 1982 to less than $80 billion in 1987; and the Saudi national budget, which had a surplus of $38 billion in 1982, was in the red by nearly $15 billion in 1987—a budget deficit proportionally four times larger than our own. But perhaps most discouraging to those American firms that export to Saudi Arabia is the rapidly shrinking market for their goods and services.

Annual spending by the Saudi government on major new projects like roadways, ports, and telecommunications projects fell from a 1982 high of $50 billion to less than $20 billion five years later. Had it not been for the Saudi government's own foreign investments the situation would have been even worse with less money available for domestic development programs. While no one is going to cry for Saudi Arabia, after it held the world ransom for more than a decade, the drop in the price of oil has put thousands of Americans out of work and cut back our sales abroad.

The rapid fall in oil prices has had disastrous secondary effects on our economy as well. The largest third world debtor nation, Brazil—which owed the world more than $115 billion in early 1987—derives much of its income from selling manufactured goods to the OPEC nations. Brazil sells vehicles to Nigeria, agricultural foodstuffs to Saudi Arabia and the Arabian Gulf nations, and weapons to nearly every country of the Middle East and Africa. Brazil's sales of trainer airplanes and heavy vehicles to OPEC countries had been a mainstay. But with OPEC nearly broke, Brazil's exports have also slumped and, without those OPEC markets, Brazil cannot pay the interest on the loans it owes to U.S. banks. Likewise, with its revenue slashed owing to OPEC's plight, Brazil is no longer a customer for our products. What has Brazil done about its loss of markets? It has done what so many other countries have done—begun selling its products cheaply inside the open markets of the United States as a partial substitute for loss of the OPEC markets. In that way, Brazil has gone from a customer to a competitor and from a growing country with a large but manageable debt to a country that is deep in recession and unable even to pay the interest on its loans to our banks. What is the final outcome? Because Brazil has entered our markets but can no longer afford to buy our products, we now have a balance-of-trade deficit with Brazil as well.

But it is not enough for Brazil to sell to the United States alone because Brazil, as the world largest third world debtor, must consistently earn large sums from its exports in order to service the interest on its debt. With programs in OPEC countries scaled back, Brazil can no longer make ends meet and the result is that this big debtor is forced to borrow even more to sustain itself. Sooner or later Brazil will give up trying to pay back its creditors or face mass uprisings since living conditions have been deteriorating as its recession continues. Today, according to the World Bank, Brazil pays out more than a third of its foreign export income to its U.S., European, and Japanese creditors, leaving little export income for its own growing population to live on. The result? Brazil, which once was the shining light of growth in Latin America, is now losing ground each year, imperiling our banks and choking off our export markets.

How does Brazil's problem affect our banks? In late February 1987, President José Sarney made the decision to suspend interest payments on the $68 billion owed to some of his country's commercial creditors (about half of Brazil's foreign debt), a decision also made by his predecessors on several occasions. Among Brazil's largest creditors are America's top five banks: Citibank, with $4.6 billion in outstanding loans to Brazil; Chase Manhattan, owed $2.8 billion; Bank of America, owed $2.7 billion; Manufacturers Hanover, $2.3 billion; and Morgan Guaranty, $1.9 billion. Each of these banks has now been forced to raise the amount of its cash reserves to protect itself from the possibility of a complete default by Brazil.

A total suspension of payments by Brazil can probably be handled by the world's banking system, although it would cause particularly large losses to some of the weaker creditors to Brazil, like Bank of America. But if two or more of the big debtor countries defaulted at roughly the same time— Mexico, Argentina, or Nigeria, for example—the impact on the world's financial system would be grave, to say the least.

SO FAR the biggest problems to have arisen in the global trading system and in the world's economy have come about not from shortages but from surpluses—contrary to the Club

of Rome's fierce predictions. We have been preparing ourselves well for shortages by investing heavily in costly stockpiles, but the world's markets are flooded with products to
sell.

It is not just changes in demand that have affected the
prices of commodities over the last three decades. In real
terms, extraction costs have also declined for the most important commodities because of improved technology. (The oil
sector is perhaps the one partial exception to the overall
decline in extraction costs because of the recent emphasis
on the lifting of oil from the ocean floor. This has led to a
two-tier cost structure for oil with dry land extraction costs
hovering between $2 and $4 per barrel—roughly 5 to 10
cents a gallon—while ocean extraction costs are closer to
$18 per barrel—about 50 cents per gallon.)

As extraction costs decline, producers have an increasingly
difficult time keeping prices up owing to factors of competition. According to the United Nations Conference on Trade
and Development's 1986 report "New Technology, Trade
and Development," the decline in extraction costs has had
a significant impact on the decline in prices for raw commodities over the last several decades. These increases in productivity in the commodity-producing sector of the economy have
meant that, in real terms, the prices for most non-fuel minerals
today are lower than they were in the early 1950s, despite
vastly increased world demand. Instead of the Club of Rome's
forecast of scarcities, we have arrived at a future in which
the prices for raw materials continue to fall, cutting into
the real incomes and buying power of the producers worldwide. This confirms that the momentary price hikes of the
1970s, when the prices of oil and other products soared,
were anomalous and based not on factors of supply or technology but on factors relating to worldwide inflation—in other
words, our mismanagement of the dollar.

As further proof that the dollar's mismanagement and not
scarcity was behind the rise in prices, let me cite the work
of Harold J. Barnett, professor emeritus of Washington University. Barnett writes in *The Resourceful Earth* that, since

1950, annual price declines in non-fuel minerals have been very significant, especially when those prices are compared to other factors in the incomes of countries around the world and when the relative value of each country's currency is also taken into account (to correct for the kind of money mismanagement that the dollar was subjected to over the last decade and a half). Looking at the figures, Barnett concludes that for the important raw materials such as iron ore, manganese ore, phosphate, aluminum, copper, lead, zinc, tin, and tungsten, prices have declined by the following annual percentages for the following countries from 1950 through 1980:

France	−.6	Japan	−2.7
Italy	−1.6	Switzerland	−3.1
Netherlands	−3.1	United States	−.3
Germany	−2.9		

For crude fertilizers, composed of phosphate rock and potash, the annual drops have been even more significant:

France	−1.0	Japan	−3.1
Italy	−1.9	Switzerland	−4.2
Netherlands	−3.4	United States	−.3
Germany	−3.3		

The above yearly averages show significant decreases in the prices of commodities over those thirty years even if we take into account the dramatic upward shifts in prices during the inflationary 1970s. And if we further factor in the large price declines in the 1980s, down a further 6.2 percent according to the U.N.'s 1986 "World Economic Survey," the figures would show even more dramatic drops in prices. For countries with stable, well-managed currencies, like Switzerland and the Netherlands, commodities cost less than half of what they did in 1950—when demand was low and stocks were plentiful.

One of the interesting features of these values is that they show that the prices for commodities in the United States and France invariably show the smallest yearly declines of any of the advanced countries (Barnett's list of countries is much longer than the one I have reproduced here). Barnett speculates in *The Resourceful Earth* that the reasons for the poor showing of the United States and France reflect the relatively poor management of these economies, compared to Japan and Germany, "especially [with respect to] foreign exchange, productivity, and inflation." While the rich European nations averaged overall yearly price drops of more than 2 percent in the prices they had to pay for commodities, our average price declines were less than .4 percent. This factor alone over the thirty-year period studied in Barnett's report means that European firms have gained significant long-term advantages over American firms in the cost of doing business owing to their better managed economies. At the same time, since so many of the commodities Barnett has studied are produced and exported by the United States, the continued and more severe drop in commodity prices suggests significantly decreased earnings for our producers in the future and a continuation of the cost advantage of non-U.S. firms over their American counterparts.

Although there has been a slight recovery in the prices of commodities since they bottomed out in mid-1986 at levels not seen since the Great Depression, the longer term outlook for domestic and international producers of fuel, non-fuel, and even agricultural commodities is not favorable. The inflated prices charged by producers during most of the 1970s and subsequent technological breakthroughs that have both lowered the cost of extraction and made substitutes available are combining to create a future in which glut, not scarcity, is the rule, to the detriment of those producer countries, including our own. Furthermore, we can infer from Barnett's figures that countries that are more heavily involved in manufacturing will continue to get the lion's share of the benefit from the declining prices of raw materials, while commodity producers will be faced with ever-dwindling purchasing power as a result of the decades-long decline in the prices they can get for their products. For countries like Japan, Germany, the Netherlands, and Switzerland, with few raw materials to export but with big manufacturing capacities, the future looks bright. For the United States, with a dwindling manufacturing sector and significantly large income derived from commodity exports, the prognosis is for a continuation of the Decline and Crash economy. Worst of all, as already mentioned, the nation's commodity producers (including oil and farm commodities) are now faced with massive debts that are putting even some of our biggest banks at risk.

Commodity gluts are not something that can be avoided; they will be with us for the foreseeable future, occasioned by the powers of technology and the forces of conservation. With our own manufacturing exports plummeting and the economic and financial profile of the United States increasingly resembling that of a third world debtor country exporting foodstuffs, ores, gold, and coal, the current raw materials glut will act as an added drag on our livelihoods. Only the most technologically advanced countries can prosper during periods of glut because efficiency and productivity are what matter most when commodities are plentiful and cheap. During those periods of oversupply what is important is how cheaply and efficiently products can be made, since no one really has a cost advantage when it comes to the prices paid for raw materials. But becoming a low-cost producer requires using our capital for long-term investment—not for stockpiling products that are already available in abundance.

Buckminster Fuller was among the first to focus the world's attention on the role technology was playing in changing the way we use commodities. Throughout his long life Fuller studied commodities in detail and their replacement by new technological processes and substitutes. During the 1930s, when Fuller worked for Phelps-Dodge, the giant American copper mining and processing company, he tried to convince people that copper, then a commodity mainstay of the US economy (not to mention the economies of Chile, Zaire, and several other third world countries), would lose much of its importance as cheaper, better substitutes came along. Unlike the Club of Rome studies a few decades later, Fuller was able to forecast correctly that new technology would drive the price of copper down in a series of stages.

Fuller was correct in his projections and in his knowledge of the cyclical way in which commodity substitutions come into use. In the earliest stages, copper wire, especially for high-tension electricity transmission, was replaced by cheaper aluminum wire. Aluminum, although not quite as good a conductor as copper, became cheaper and more plentiful when new smelting and refining processes were developed in the 1920s. Copper usage began to decline until the advent of World War II, when it again assumed a leading role in the war effort as the ideal material from which to make shell casings. Once the war ended, though, the replacement of copper wire with aluminum began in earnest around the country.

However, the market that was lost in the high-tension electrical transmission sector was soon replaced by the newer, growing telephone market. And even with competition from aluminum, copper prices could sustain an increase of about 30 percent between 1950 and 1970 owing to the expansion of its use to the growing worldwide telephone systems. But this was the end of big demand and high prices for copper.

By 1970, technologies of a radically new design were developed. These new technologies would make the use of copper in telephone lines obsolete. For example, in the 1970s, large communications satellites were launched that could link Europe with the United States. Each of these new satellites, comprising less than a ton of silicon, plastic, gold, some copper, and other exotic metals and alloys, replaced at least one undersea copper cable (and sometimes several) weighing tens of thousands of tons. What's more, these old cables, some dating back to the 1920s, could not carry data as efficiently as satellites and could not handle the rapidly growing volume of calls between Europe and the United States. This meant that copper lost its role in voice and data transmission not because demand for the service it provided was slipping, but because demand grew so fast it initiated a whole new phase in technological development.

In the 1970s fiber optics also became a commercially available substitute for copper capable of carrying both voice and data transmission with features vastly superior to those of copper. Some fiber-optic cables are capable of carrying as many as sixteen thousand simultaneous transmissions, while the best copper cable is only able to carry a dozen or so simultaneous transmissions. Fiber optics also has a big cost advantage over copper since it is composed primarily of high-silica-content sand, which is readily available. Today, nearly all new undersea cables are made of fiber-optic material and copper cables have become obsolete. As a result of these new technological developments, between 1970 and 1980 the price of copper declined by almost 40 percent.

But the copper cables in the sea beds and the miles of copper wire formerly used to link telephones and computers did not vanish out of existence because of these new technologies. Millions of tons of refined, high-grade ore are now suddenly available to any company with the ability to recover and recycle the ore. Most of the world's copper mines, which were developed over the centuries at tremendous cost in both human life and capital, are now superfluous owing to the massive quantities of copper that lie in storage aboveground. According to Philip K. Verleger, Jr., visiting fellow at the Institute for International Economics and one of the world's foremost commodity market experts, "one of the biggest potential suppliers of copper isn't a new mine in Chile, but the old wire cables under the streets of New York City" (*Development Business,* May 31, 1987). With limited demand for new copper, Verleger believes "the demand for basic commodities will be weak for the foreseeable future." If Verleger is correct, then our bankers have a lot to worry about.

Tin is also rapidly becoming obsolete. As Buckminster Fuller was fond of pointing out in his lectures, during World War II, when airplane manufacturing reached all-time highs, the dies used to make the aluminum parts of the fighters, bombers, and troop transports were made of tin from the mines of Malaysia, China, and Brazil. Several million tons of this very high grade refined ore still remain at airplane factories and at airfields around the country. Even today, this stockpile greatly exceeds the annual usage of the metal and, if needed, could provide us with all of our tin needs well into the future, much to the dismay of tin-producing countries around the world.

But our tin needs have been declining just as our usage of copper has been declining. Tin, most familiar to us as a coating for cans, is rapidly being replaced by new food-preservation technologies. Plastics, new types of coated fiber, extremely thin aluminum sheet, and the widespread use of frozen food all have cut into tin's traditional markets. The transformation of the American Can Company—once the world's largest maker of tin cans—into Primerica, a diversified financial services company that no longer has any interests in the packaging business, illustrates how times have changed. With the tin can no longer dominating packaging, the price for this once important metal has hit an all-time low.

The average car now uses 20 percent less steel than it did in the 1950s just as worldwide steel capacity has expanded. No wonder our midwestern iron ore is selling at depressed prices. Mines in Brazil, Colombia, Canada, and Australia are also fighting it out for market share.

Aircraft are now being built with less aluminum but more plastic and carbon-fiber composites. So severe has the slump been in aluminum prices that many refiners have temporarily shut down until demand picks up.

Automobile engines, now made of cast iron, will soon have a greater proportion of their parts made from new ceramic materials, which, like fiber optics, are mostly silica. True to form, the Japanese are already in the lead, with ceramic turbo chargers now included on a number of production models.

What this means is that one material will no longer simply be substituted for another, in an easy one-for-one equation. Rather, technology has made available a wide range of substitutes for inclusion into new products. Automobiles may use 20 percent less steel today, and even less tomorrow, but they will be composed of more types of alloys, plastics and fibers, and composites than ever before.

For manufacturers the news is good because it means that the price and availability of no single commodity will dominate the cost of production as in the past. For commodity producers the news means a loss of clout and an increase in competition from other producers. This, in turn, means less opportunity to build up OPEC-like cartels that can keep prices artificially high.

The trend toward greater diversity in the use of raw materials by manufacturers also spells bad news for those countries that specialize in producing only one commodity. These countries will have to broaden their production base to include other commodities. But branching out to produce other goods will have an impact on other markets as well, which may also lead to gluts.

Taken together, the trend in commodity usage points in a direction completely opposite to that indicated by the Club of Rome. For producers, and for their creditors, the trend is toward lower earnings.

Malaysia is the world's largest tin-exporting nation. It has embarked upon a new strategy for the future after having failed to revive the depressed tin market. Like other commodity producers, Malaysia is heavily in debt and must maintain a rapid growth rate to pay back the loans it owes to our banks and to improve its standard of living. To do this, Malaysia has decided to move quickly into the high-tech area and is now host to dozens of American and Japanese multinationals, particularly those that produce integrated circuit components. Today, our companies are taking advantage of Malaysia's cheap labor, and Malaysian workers are beginning to learn modern manufacturing techniques. Through joint ventures and with the establishment of Malaysian venture capital companies, this well-located Asian country has now become the world's largest exporter of integrated circuits and silicon components. Home-grown Malaysian electronics companies are starting to crop up and in time they will become competitors to our own firms. With the aid of the Japanese, Malaysia will begin building an automobile, the "Proton," for export and will soon be selling that car in the United States.

What does this mean for us? As Malaysia and other commodity producers are confronted with situations of chronic oversupply, they will do everything they can to become manufacturing countries. As these countries make the transition, they will utilize their low-paid labor forces to gain access to our open markets. As we retreat from manufacturing, these nations will move in to fill the void—especially since their traditional exports are depressed. And as they succeed in the manufacturing arena, they will soon become rich enough to compete in other areas as well. What will that mean to us? Simply that our losses to foreign competition will grow as our own incomes continue on their downward slide. While the Club of Rome focused our attention on the quantities of resources in the world, we should have been examining the truly serious scarcities that were developing—the declining number of American companies manufacturing products both for domestic consumption and for the export market. And the numbers grow fewer each year.

9

SLUGGING IT OUT FOR MARKET SHARE IN A WORLD OF TOO MUCH INDUSTRIAL CAPACITY

OVERCAPACITY is not limited to the raw materials sector of the economy. The phenomenal growth of trade and investment during the post–World War II years through the late 1970s enhanced both our ability to extract resources from the ground and our ability to produce goods. The same multinational companies that took our manufacturing capacity and distributed it throughout the world in search of cheaper labor supplies also greatly accelerated the growth of trade by transferring these products between their various local and domestic divisions.

Multinationalism, as practiced by such pioneering companies as ITT, Honeywell, Borg-Warner, Chrysler, Firestone, Ford, Dupont, Union Carbide, and others, enabled worldwide trade in manufactured goods to grow at 11 percent per year between 1950 and 1975—just prior to the onset of the Decline and Crash. This means that total world trade in manufactured products like cars, radios, ships, and airplanes doubled every seven or eight years, infusing the world's markets with more goods of better quality than ever before. Trade in general, during this same period, was growing nearly as rapidly, doubling every ten or eleven years, meaning that overall world output was increasing at astronomical rates and pulling millions of people throughout the world from the depths of poverty and into the middle class. This great expansion of the world's economy developed in an orderly way under U.S. tutelage, and it is something that Americans should be proud of.

During these pro-growth years, trade was facilitated by stable exchange rates and low interest rates and the agency of the multinational corporation. During this period the entire world was lifted out of the rubble left over from World War II and the Great Depression. Instead of the market gluts we face today, there were widespread shortages of everything from autos to wheat. As the world's largest exporter, we were able to produce goods and supply raw materials to make up for shortages elsewhere. And as the world's largest importer, our hunger for the world's output stimulated the economies of dozens of countries.

To a significant degree trade still drives economic growth. But since 1978 annual growth in world trade has barely nudged above 3 percent, with some years showing big declines. During the 1980s, which have been characterized by a wildly fluctuating dollar, rising and falling interest rates, massive trade deficits, oceans of American and third world debt, flagging U.S. productivity growth, and a world wide oversupply of most commodities, world trade has been either contracting or remaining flat.

But to say that trade remained flat during the 1980s is misleading. In fact, the only reason the trade figures for the world have shown any growth at all during the last decade is because of the Decline and Crash of our economy. Our massive importation of foreign goods during the Reagan years coupled with our gigantic trade deficit is the only reason the overall figures for world trade do not show a far greater contraction. The big appetite of the American people, coupled with our dwindling ability to provide for ourselves, has been the only barrier to a full-scale trade collapse. The price for acting as the world's major market has been the transformation of our nation from net creditor to net debtor. Japan and the European countries may have been able to avert major downturns in their economies at home, thanks to our open markets and our run-up of debt, but we are the ones who have been left with the bill. How will that bill be paid? Through greater reductions in our standard of living in the years to come.

We acted to stimulate the economies of Europe and Japan, our major competitors as well as our major trading partners, but we have done little to revive the fortunes of those countries that now comprise our own major markets—clearly a wrongheaded strategy.

After Canada, the largest markets for our goods lie in the third world. But as luck would have it, the third world has been in the midst of a deep recession, even a depression in some countries, since about 1980, largely because of the current glut in raw materials. As a result, the third world, despite its rapidly growing population, has all but ceased to be a market for our goods. Although economic growth in the developed world increased by an average of about 1 percent per year during the period 1980–1985, growth in the third world during the same period came to a virtual halt, with many economies in that region actually shrinking. Overall averages are misleading, however, since a few third world countries, such as Korea, Taiwan, Malaysia, and Thailand, accounted for just about all of the region's slim gains through increased purchases by the United States of their manufactured goods.

For the majority of the third world the Reagan years have been a time of suffering, scaled-back living standards, and drops in foreign purchases. For instance, from 1980 through 1987, Africa's average income per person fell 11 percent, Latin America's and the Caribbean's per capita income fell 7.5 percent, and the Middle East saw a dramatic 19.2 percent collapse in per capita earnings. For the poor of the world, who have little to begin with, these declines in income have meant cutbacks in the necessities of life. The cessation of growth in the third world has also meant that the region's middle class, which began to emerge in countries like Mexico during the early 1970s, has already begun to shrink. For those families that were on the verge of joining this new middle class, the resumption of an existence on the borderline of poverty is accompanied by mounting frustrations and deep resentments.

As a result of the large contractions in the economies of the third world, there has been a sharp decrease in the overall buying power of the citizens there. At the same time, these declines have meant that the gap between people living in the world's rich countries and those in the world's poor countries has widened markedly during the 1980s. According to a special survey in *South* magazine (January 1987): "the gap between the average citizen in the industrialized group [of countries] and his counterpart in the developing world has grown still wider. A quarter century ago, the average citizen in the non-Communist North [the industrialized countries of the United States, Europe, and Japan] was 20 times better off than the average in low-income regions like India, Bangladesh, and much of Africa. By the late 1970s the figure was 40 times. Now, according to World Bank data, it is 46 times." With such large declines, the prospects for reviving one of our biggest markets appears bleak, especially when we consider that the prices for our products have in no way retreated from their inflation-bloated highs of the seventies and early eighties. Consider how many four-wheel-drive jeeps we will sell to a depressed third world when they now cost between $15,000 and $20,000 and must compete with new Japanese, Korean, Brazilian, and soon even Malaysian rivals costing only a quarter as much.

Even the richest third world markets are not able to keep pace with the increases in the rest of the world. Twenty-five years ago in the richer developing countries like Brazil, Egypt, and Malaysia, the income gap between their citizens and those of the developed countries was one dollar to every seven. Now, for every dollar earned in the richer developing countries, nine are earned by those in the North. Outside of Korea and the other booming third world countries, overall investment in the South has declined by more than 30 percent since the late 1970s. This decline in investment means that incomes in the region are not likely to recover, and there aren't likely to be any increases in third world purchases of American goods.

For American companies that have bet heavily on the third world as major purchasers of our goods, the growth statistics of these countries are a disaster. Not only that, but the depression affecting the third world has forced them to try and export their products to our markets, often at bargain basement prices. To contend with the currently depressed market for commodities, the most vigorous and resilient economies of the third world have already developed a substantial trade in manufactured goods among themselves that is not limited to just textiles, steel, and cars, but includes more sophisticated goods as well. As the expertise of the third world develops, these countries will begin to compete with us in our other markets.

Developing countries have been trying to make the shift from heavy dependence on commodity exports to greater reliance on manufactured exports for at least a decade. They have been prodded and primed for the transition by the writings of the late Argentinian economist Raul Prebisch, who showed in the January 1987 *South* magazine that after a recession the prices of manufactured goods recover more than those of commodities. In this analysis, which applies to both developed as well as developing producers, the commodity provider will continue to lose ground to the manufacturer, which accounts for the growing gap between incomes in the developed and developing worlds.

From our point of view, Prebisch's theory means that the markets of our goods in the third world will continue to decline. At the same time, because many developing countries are trying to industrialize, the market for manufactured products will also face greater levels of oversupply, further complicating the picture.

The exports of manufactured goods produced in the third world still come from only a handful of countries, most of which are located in Asia. These countries have been quite sophisticated in their approach to entering our market. While we may have devalued our dollar against European and the Japanese currencies by as much as 40 percent, in a vain effort to cut out balance-of-trade deficit, most developing countries have let their currencies fall along with ours. That means that imports of Korean, Brazilian, Taiwanese, and Malaysian goods are now no more expensive to the American consumers than they were before the dollar dropped, whereas the prices for products produced by European and Japanese firms have begun to climb.

Our policy with respect to imports is a little like our policy in the Persian Gulf. Just as we sent our warships into the Gulf before we checked for mines, we also lowered the value of the dollar before we checked to see if we could replace our imports with domestically made products. Tragically, there are far too few American-made products that can replace foreign consumer products and increasingly even foreign-made capital goods like machine tools. As Japanese VCRs have gone up in price, owing to the falling dollar, the prices of Korean models have remained unchanged because they have not let the value of their currencies rise. Add to this pegging of Korean and Taiwanese currencies the additional fact that we no longer make the products that we import and it is easy to see why our trade gap has persisted despite the 40 percent devaluation of our currency.

As we make the shift from purchasing Japanese goods to buying products from Korea, Mexico, and Brazil, we should be seeing some benefits as these countries turn around and buy the products that we still do make, like computers and new passenger jets. But that will not be the case. Countries like Brazil use their earnings to pay back their loans, not to buy our products. Others, like Korea and the Asian developing nations, are now so tightly linked to Japan that they have all but ceased buying what we make. For these reasons, the trade deficits we have with these developing countries have not been whittled away. As a result, we no longer derive much benefit from our trading relations with these countries outside of our access to their cheap manufactured goods.

Even though the third world remains in a state of economic stagnation, the competition for what business remains is heating up. Japanese, German, and even high-wage Swedish firms are making inroads into what was once an exclusively American market. Oil-rich Mexico, with its close proximity to the United States and its traditional reliance on the United States for such products as autos, trucks, and locomotives, has been invaded by other countries that are selling their products made half a world away at prices well below those of American firms operating just north of the border. In Mexico and the other developing countries, GM, Mack, and Ford trucks are being replaced by the higher quality products from Volvo, Mercedes, and Hino while Volkswagen, Nissan, and Toyota take over the car markets. In those depressed markets, foreign manufacturers are also willing to accept payment through elaborate barter schemes whereby Mexican oil is traded for trucks or Brazilian hardwood, rubber, and paper are traded for machine tools.

Japanese electronics firms have rushed into those niches of the market abandoned by venerable American firms like RCA, GE, and Zenith while Korean clones of IBM PCs crowd out the originals in third world markets just as they are doing here at home. The Japanese and Europeans are getting very successful in the third world because they are taking a much longer view than we are. Europeans and Japanese also give a great deal of foreign aid to the developing world in ways that will later win them projects (for instance, the Japanese donated a television studio and station to the island nation of Sri Lanka, to help Japanese electronics firms like Sony sell TV sets in that market). British foreign aid can be used by developing countries with only one catch—it must be used to purchase British products and hire British consultants, who in large part advise the developing countries to buy more British products and hire more British consultants. At the World Bank and the other international development banks that dole out more than $37 billion in project funds per year to the third world, American firms have fallen from first to third place in the number of contracts they win for this overseas work. Because American firms are garnering fewer of these fat contracts, even though Congress is the largest funder of the international development organizations, the banks themselves have launched an offensive to find American companies that can carry out projects. In most cases, though, the firms they find simply are not interested in exporting, even though our trade deficit continues to grow. According to one bank official, while salesmen from European and Japanese companies are frequent guests at the Inter-American Development Bank's Washington headquarters, American firms seldom make the visit despite the urging of our government.

India is a good example of how we have failed to look to the future. While American firms sat back appalled at India's poverty, the Japanese looked long term—aided by the high-quality studies produced by the Japanese government's Institute for Developing Economies—and quietly took over India's telephone, automobile, motorcycle, and scooter industries. India, with a population of 750 million, may not offer significant profits today, but it has a great deal of potential for the future. It has been able to boost its agricultural output and, while still very poor by our standards, it already has the third largest university system in the world and one of the most highly developed scientific research systems anywhere. For a country that is still living in poverty, its well-developed university system has trained many world-class Indian scientists—especially in engineering, biology, and computer sciences—who will help that country grow in the future. Today India is a weak market but it will not remain so. And as it grows, and as its 750 million citizens become richer, the Japanese will already be firmly entrenched.

What this means in the long term is that when (and if) the third world finally recovers from its economic collapse and becomes a viable market we may play only a very small supporting role in the economic drama now being written by the more future oriented Europeans and Japanese. The prize for thinking decades ahead? A vast third world market comprising more than two-thirds of humanity!

Today, largely as a result of the loss of the valuable third world market, there is a global glut of almost every type of good that we and our competitors produce. Global overcapacity in nearly every industry exists at the same time as the markets themselves have shrunk. Within this climate of shrinking markets, it is hard to convince American business leaders that the only way we can continue to exist as a high-wage, manufacturing country is if industry invests large sums of money in automation to increase productivity and lower costs dramatically, thereby increasing their overall market share. If American market share grows, then overall employment in this sector can remain even as automation increases productivity. This is the case in Japan where employment in manufacturing remains high despite automation.

For most managers, faced with current rates of overcapacity in their industries, the typical solution has been to cut capacity by shutting down the most outdated and high-cost plants, primarily those located in the United States, and shift production to cheaper offshore sites. Few managers, outside of Japan, would have the courage and foresight to invest in automation and other productivity enhancers during times of glut in an effort to become more efficient, lower cost producers. Automating is an expensive proposition fraught with risks. Companies that attempt it are ridiculed by the press and lambasted by their investors—most of whom think no more than six months into the future. Just consider how destructively investors and the business press have treated GM's chairman Roger Smith as he fights to modernize, integrate, and automate GM's vast manufacturing operations. At the same time they have praised his recent decision to close parts-producing operations and import more components from abroad. Not only are they critical of his ambitious plans, but because the giant automaker's earnings momentarily dipped below those of Ford, critics say GM's efforts to become the world's lowest cost, highest quality auto company are simply folly. The verdict is far from rendered, but greedy stockholders and critics with no sense of the future may yet sabotage one of the best thought out (and costly—$40 billion) attempts to keep America at the cutting edge of manufacturing and technology. Consider what automating GM will mean to our economy in the long run as exports from car makers in such emerging cheap labor countries as Taiwan, Malaysia, Brazil, and even the Soviet Union begin to invade our shores.

Because the third world has effectively ceased to be a market for our goods and in many cases is now a competitor, we must either help to revive that part of the world's purchasing power or we must begin to look elsewhere if we are to resurrect our industry and gain a favorable balance of trade. But without the third world, there is no "elsewhere" to look. There is currently far more industrial capacity available in the world than is required to fulfill the needs of the rich countries alone. Today, with so much excess capacity, the growth of one firm or one country can only come at the expense of another, and the competition is intense.

In ancient times there were ways to forgive debt when the economy of a nation became bogged down. Yet today we do not have such mechanisms. And by forcing the third world to meet its financial obligations—to support the profits of our banks—we may be placing ourselves in a situation that is actually worse than if a plan were worked out to forgive the third world's debt and assure that they will once again become purchasers of our products.

How bad is the current level of global industrial overcapacity? According to a number of analyses, including one by the *Wall Street Journal* on March 3, 1987, with the third world in the midst of a deep depression the world now has at least 20 percent too much industrial capacity, with some industries in even worse shape. With so much excess capacity, prices are forced down, profits are slumping, and companies are hesitating to invest. Let us examine the situation in the most important industrial sectors:

Autos. According to the *Wall Street Journal,* yearly world demand for cars is currently hovering at about 30 million.

Yet because of the available worldwide capacity, current annual production capacity is at about the 40–45 million level. That means that current global annual overcapacity is running about 10–15 million units, about 25 percent of total production. And more capacity is currently being added in Asia, where the home market is still small, and in North America and Latin America.

In the auto industry, nothing seems to be stopping the addition of new capacity and most companies are operating under the assumption that they can garner enough of the market to operate profitably. While GM and Ford have been laying off American workers by the tens of thousands over the last five years, Japanese auto companies are in the process of building new U.S. factories for their cars. When the Japanese have finished adding to their current U.S. capacity, they will be able to assemble an additional 1.4 million new cars for the American market each year, a market that has by all measures stopped growing. Unless demand suddenly swells, those new cars will remain unsold or will displace cars built by Detroit.

The Japanese may be thinking of adding to their U.S. capacity so that they can cut down their exports and free up some plant capacity in Japan. But freeing up plant capacity in Japan means that cars made there will be shipped and sold somewhere else, because the Japanese home market is not growing. In any event, more Japanese capacity, whether here or abroad, means more automobile gluts, during which time only the most efficient (or best subsidized) producers will survive. So bad is the current level of overcapacity in the auto industry that many European manufacturers would be forced out of business if it were not for the subsidies that are given to them by their governments as schemes for boosting employment.

Steel. Accurate estimates of steel overcapacity are difficult to make, but it appears that in today's global market there are at least 100–150 million and perhaps even as much as 200 million metric tons of excess capacity. According to John Jacobson, an economist with Chase Econometrics, who is

quoted in the *Wall Street Journal* analysis, current worldwide
overcapacity is now roughly equal to total U.S. steel-produc-
ing capacity. But more capacity will soon be forthcoming.
If the United States were to go out of the steel business entirely
(as we sometimes seem to be doing), then worldwide supply
and demand would be in equilibrium. In spite of the glut
of steel, Brazil and Korea are building huge new plants for
the export market, as are other countries. But at whose expense will this steel be sold as it pours into an already glutted
market? We must ask ourselves if we really are ready to
invest in truly state-of-the-art automated steel production,
or if we wish to purchase even more of this vital metal from
abroad.

Computers. While factory orders for new computers
plunged 15 percent during the 1984–1986 period, with IBM
particularly hard hit, manufacturers of peripheral equipment,
particularly in the Far East, have started to produce entire
systems. Accurate estimates of computer overcapacity are
difficult to make, but it is generally believed to be highly
significant. Korean clones of IBM PCs, Japanese laptops and
mainframes, and new German and French mainframes
threaten to flood the world market with computers that cannot be sold at a profit. Such a condition would starve our
companies of vital investment and research funds that they
need to compete in the future.

Semiconductors. The *Wall Street Journal* states that the
U.S. and Japanese semiconductor industries together produce
86 percent of the world's chips. Production equipment usage
in these two countries is running at only about 70 percent
of capacity. Even if we exclude the venerable, but smaller,
European producers and the newer low-cost producers in
Malaysia, it seems that current worldwide overcapacity in
this "sunrise industry" is about a third more than demand.
Soon Brazil and Korea will be in the semiconductor business,
adding even more capacity to the global market.

Heavy Equipment. The farm gluts plaguing the United
States and Europe, and the astronomical levels of indebtedness
among American farmers, have been hurting the heavy equip-

ment manufacturers for years. Worldwide tractor production fell from 230,000 units in 1979 to 120,000 in 1986. Worldwide production of large tractors, over 100 horsepower, sunk from 80,000 units in 1979 to barely 20,000 units in1986. According to the *Wall Street Journal,* sluggish demand for heavy equipment means that today there is 40 percent overcapacity around the world. Surprisingly, with the exception of farm equipment, low-cost producers, particularly in Korea, are continuing to add to worldwide capacity in an effort to grab an increased market share while American firms build new, cheap labor plants in Mexico and Asia. With no recovery in this market in sight, and with more capacity forthcoming, there may be an even bigger shift of American production abroad.

Textiles. According to the *Wall Street Journal,* "overcapacity lingers on as more and more mills are being built in less developed nations," turning our highest cost domestic plants into surplus capacity. Domestic plants have been closed and there has been a loss of about 700,000 jobs at home as a result, while companies continue to build new plants around the world. As a result of overcapacity and cheap foreign labor, the share of U.S. textile imports has increased from 25 percent of the total U.S. market in 1980 to an all-time high of 55 percent today.

Worldwide, there seems to be a rough equilibrium between supply and demand only in the chemical, pharmaceutical, and, not surprisingly, weapons industries. This may simply reflect the high cost of entering these markets, with their emphasis on world-class research, highly trained personnel, and, for the most part, production that is capital intensive.

As long as we are plagued by overcapacity and shrinking markets we will be struggling with our trading partners not for new markets but simply for market share. In view of the glut in manufactured goods, prices may be driven down and factories closed in a situation analogous to what is happening with respect to commodities. Today's crowded markets, whether in real estate, commodities, transportation, or manufacturing, are forcing many firms to the sidelines and prodding those that remain to cut their overhead and lower their production costs.

One way to keep the competition out is to protect our home market. We could also put pressure on our third world clients to close their doors to anyone but our firms. But these days such strong-arm tactics would spell disaster. Too much of the world's economy is currently kept afloat by the appetite of the American consumer. No matter that all our purchases are made on time, we are the only big purchaser left in the game, and for that reason the world is willing to lend us the money we need to buy their products. If we closed our markets to foreigners during this period of glut, the shock waves would rattle through Europe and Japan. Retaliations would surely ensue, and the world would be thrown headlong into a depression of momentous proportions sparked by the collapse of trade during a full-blown trade war—a replay of what happened in 1929. This is especially true after the stock market crash of October 1987, which left the international financial markets in a condition of nervousness and extreme vulnerability. To close our markets to foreigners while we restore the "competitiveness" of our industry would pull down what is left of the great post–World War II system. Besides, experience has shown that when our markets are protected, American firms use that breathing space not to become more competitive but to raise prices and go into other businesses that are often import related.

What is needed is not to protect our markets jealously, although we could do a lot more to aid our new and emerging companies and our strategic industries, but rather to reopen closed markets. The sooner the third world resumes its growth, the quicker will our overcapacity be absorbed.

It may be many years before the third world once again goes on a buying spree, and those companies that can hold on the longest, in light of the global glut, will be the ones that will prosper when (and if) the third world reemerges. To ride out this condition of overcapacity requires tremendous foresight and nerves of steel, as well as sympathetic investors willing to sit through periods of losses while investment is made in new technology. In America, needless to say, the investors are hardly sympathetic.

When it comes to patience the Europeans will probably fare best. European governments have a big stake in keeping their industries afloat and retaining production at home. They would never allow the kind of predatory destruction of an industry such as happened in the United States to the airline industry after deregulation when Eastern, Continental, People's Express, National, Western, Piedmont, and TWA were either absorbed or bought out at bargain prices. Nor would they be inclined to allow the kind of chaos we lived with during the airline wars. European businesses operate in an environment that is much more regulated. Even when government-owned companies in Europe were "privatized" to increase competition, it was done in a way that was more orderly than we have come to expect. One of the reasons for this is that European companies are bound by rules that make it difficult and expensive to fire people.

The Europeans, outside of the Soviet bloc, have a large share of nationalized industries, and governments can continue pumping money into losing businesses as long as they provide jobs and votes. Some of the most venerable nameplates in the industrial world are produced by companies in which the government holds a large stake: BMW, Renault, Airbus Industries, Volkswagen, Rolls Royce, British Telecom, British Steel, Fiat, Dassault, Aerospatiale, SAS, Thomson electronics, to name a few. In the fight for market share, should any of these major companies undergo real damage, it is a foregone conclusion that they will be kept afloat by their governments.

The labor unions in Europe, with their direct links to political parties, have the kind of clout necessary to keep European firms afloat during bad times. European governments are not averse to nationalizations and to the kinds of loan guarantees we gave to Lockheed and Chrysler that required much soul searching here. Repeatedly, nationalizations have been used as a way to protect against job loss and to ensure the continuity of a company. In this way, the European system can assure the survival of its industries, but usually at a great cost in efficiency, even in the most crowded market.

Many European governments have gained a great deal of experience over the years by taking over ailing companies, nurturing them back to health, and then selling them off— all without a pang of guilt. The British government recently accomplished such a rescue job with Jaguar, which was suffering tremendous losses while producing cars of very dubious quality. Through careful husbanding of the company, the government was able to nurse Jaguar back to health and finally to profitability before returning it to the private sector through a sale of government-owned shares. For other industries operating in overcrowded markets, such as shipbuilding, steel making, and mining, European governments have succeeded in protecting jobs but have not been able to bring about recoveries. Only Germany and Norway can build ships profitably in Europe, although the British and Swedish governments still subsidize their shipyards, hoping to return them eventually to health.

The Japanese also have an advantage compared to U.S. companies when it comes to coping with sustained periods of glut. Japanese firms are capitalized, and often owned in large part, not by private or institutional investors but by the leading Japanese banks. Banks in Japan seek consistent, rather than spectacular, earnings over the long haul. For a Japanese bank a long-term relationship with a major multinational company can be very profitable and very safe. These banks can afford to lend money in bad times because they can exert a large measure of control over management and even require the company to use the banks' other services. Japanese firms, fighting to keep or increase their market share, can absorb a 40 percent appreciation of the yen against the dollar while only modestly increasing the prices of their products because their banks do not require the kind of earnings our shareholders do. Japanese companies can even afford to dump their products onto the world markets, often at significant losses, to gain or retain market share because banks are not institutional investors looking only for higher profits.

Big Japanese companies also have stockholders, but generally they are far friendlier to the long-term aspirations of a company. Like all stockholders, Japanese investors want to see the value of their shares appreciate—and they have. But because Japanese interest and inflation rates are low, Japanese investors do not complain if a company has a very high price/earnings ratio. This means a stock can maintain its value even with reduced profits.

The price/earnings ratio is generally considered to be a guide for determining how well a company is managed. But different cultures read the price/earnings ratio differently.

The price/earnings ratio is figured in two steps. First, the earnings of the company are divided by the number of outstanding shares. Then this figure is divided by the price of an individual share. If a company has earnings of $10,000,000 and has 100,000 shares outstanding which sell for $5 then its price/earnings ratio is 20/1 ($10,000,000 divided by 100,000 divided by 5 = 20).

In the U.S. market, investors require low P/E ratios. A typical stock must have a value less than 20 for it to retain its standing in the market. Only a few American stocks can retain their market value with P/E ratios above 20/1. Japanese investors, however, tolerate P/E ratios of 50/1, or even more, before a stock loses its appeal. That means that a typical investor on the Tokyo exchange is satisfied with a company that has more outstanding shares or earns less per share than an American company. If a Japanese company can sell more shares than an American company and still retain its value, then it can use the extra capital it receives for those added shares for its own investment purposes.

Companies with stocks that can retain their value even with high P/E ratios have a big advantage over companies that cannot. For instance, these companies can afford to invest heavily in new technology and in new research—expenditures which typically cut deeply into a firm's profits. Companies with high ratios can also afford the cost of opening new markets, making long-term plans and operating under conditions of fluctuating currency values. So far, in the United States pharmaceutical companies are about the only companies with high P/Es tolerated by investors. Typically, pharmaceutical companies are research intensive, forward looking, and well managed—the typical profile of a large Japanese firm. And when a pharmaceutical firm comes out with a new and successful product, investors know very well that the product will be able to support the company for years to come. While we allow only pharmaceutical firms to operate under these optimum conditions—with good results, since they are still among our most competitive companies—the Japanese allow all their firms the luxury of high P/E ratios.

Both Japanese and European firms have advantages over American firms in being able to sit out a global recession and in the fight for market share. In the United States, if a major company's earnings dip, even if it is caused by increased research and investment, its stock price usually flounders— an open invitation to a corporate raider. The plethora of raiders inhabiting Wall Street has turned the management of even the largest companies jittery. Increasingly, vital investment capital has been squandered not on productivity increases but on buybacks of a company's stock. (This was especially the case when the Dow took its 508-point plunge in October 1987.) Even GM, frightened at its drop in earnings, has announced plans to acquire billions of dollars' worth of its own shares. And GM is not alone in having to focus significant resources on fighting the predatory practices of the takeover specialists, instead of riding out the long-term crisis in the global market. Dozens of companies have scaled back investment and research plans to enable them to devote large sums of money to acquiring more of their own shares.

Even if takeovers were outlawed, American firms, on their own and wedded to the fluctuating stock market, would still be victimized by big institutional traders. These traders may buy a stock for a pension fund and then threaten to leave that stock, and let it fall, if earnings, even in the shortest term, are not high enough. To many fund managers it makes no difference how the company maintains those earnings.

Closing manufacturing plants in the United States and moving production offshore has pleased many fund managers interested only in short-term return, as has the transformation of companies from manufacturing giants into marketing or financial services firms. When American Can transformed itself from the world's largest manufacturer of containers into a financial services company, few of the investing fund managers made a fuss because Jerry Tsai, the CEO who masterminded the change, was able to keep earnings high. Litton Industries, which once manufactured office equipment and pioneered the microwave oven, now imports its ovens and concerns itself primarily with financial services. As long as earnings are high, most fund managers could care less about the day-to-day activities of the company—and the country—because their interest is in short-term earnings. If a company falters, they can desert it with one phone call, but if the company decides to invest in its future, the fund managers are almost certain to desert it because of a short-term dip in earnings.

BY THE year 2000, just moments away, really, the world's population will have vaulted over the 7 billion mark. Of these 7 billion, more than half will be under thirty years of age, with two-thirds of them living in the debt-plagued third world. For the industrialized countries, these new faces could be the answer to current overcapacity. Without their purchasing and producing capabilities fully engaged, the Decline and Crash may accelerate and become an all-out slugfest for market share.

If these were rational times, led by rational, concrete thinkers, men and women who value the real, tangible wealth of the country, the biggest challenge would be to mastermind a strategy for bringing the third world back into the world economy, just as Europe and Japan were brought back after World War II. If the third world were growing economically, not just with respect to its population, it just might herald the start of a long period of economic expansion analogous to that in the United States, Europe, and Japan during the postwar baby boom years.

After all, each person born on our planet, here or in the third world, needs housing, schools, clean water, electricity, a place to work, and the infrastructure for support. Today, with its huge $1 trillion debt burden and its stalled economy, the third world has curtailed its imports and let its infrastructure deteriorate.

If real growth returned to this part of the world, at levels as great as those in the mid-1970s, third world governments and private sector firms would once again become big markets for our goods and services, doing much to reverse the ill effects of the Decline and Crash.

When it comes to the third world debt problem, the only people making any noise are the bankers, those short-sighted businessmen who created the problem in the first place by making billions in dubious loans. At the same time, our companies are clamoring for new markets because they are unable to sell to the third world. But the banks are interested only in pressing for full payment of their loans; they are not interested in developing realistic ways to ease the pressure on the third world. As a result, commodity gluts persist while huge markets for our goods remain behind locked doors and nations struggle to pay off their debts. It is a vicious circle.

The crisis confronting capitalism is the crisis of overproduction. It need not be so. The crisis of overproduction can be swept away when the third world becomes a purchaser again. If this happens and production picks up, demand for the third world's commodities will also increase.

10

PICKING UP
THE PIECES:
A PRESCRIPTION FOR
RENEWAL

NO ONE likes to be the harbinger of bad news, least of all
me. To be sure, there are some few bright spots in the economy
where we still retain some measure of overall leadership,
such as in aerospace, the high-technology medical and pharmaceutical fields, and in biotechnology. But we must act
decisively to undo fifteen years of economic lunacy during
which time debts have mounted, incomes have shrunk, and
the nation as a whole has grown weaker. We must also change
our business climate to make productive investment worthwhile and takeovers difficult and to protect our vital equity
from foreign purchase. We must do something to raise the
wages and ease the economic burden of the average American
worker.

The magic of the market and the invisible hand have both
worked well in this country to propel us from an agricultural
backwater at the end of the nineteenth century to the world's
dominant, but declining, economic power today. But the invisible hand has worked less well here than planning has in

other countries. France, Japan, and Sweden have all exceeded our growth rates and raised themselves from poverty to equal or better our standard of living in little more than half the time it took for us to make our own meteoric rise—and they made their gains without our rich resource deposits and plentiful farmland. Italy, which has adopted a strange blend of planning and a free market that borders on anarchy, has grown so fast of late that it is now threatening to overtake Great Britain in per capita income. Needless to say, Great Britain, which has had a stagnant economy for decades, shares our prejudice against planning. Of the advanced, developed countries in the world, the United States and Britain are the ones with the worst slums.

As I mentioned previously, there are two kinds of planning—push and pull. Push planning, the kind adopted by the Soviet Union and Eastern European countries, has consistently failed in every sector except the military. Push planning, where a bureaucrat determines the quotas of various products to be produced, tries to be much too encompassing. Push planning aims at taking control of every minor detail of the economy and as a result fails miserably because it does not allow for innovation, enterprise, or creativity. It simply commands managers and workers into action, thus violating their freedom of choice and limiting their options. We must all give thanks that this type of heavy-handed planning appears to be on its way out not just in the Soviet Union, but in Eastern Europe, China, and in a number of third world countries as well.

Then there is pull planning. This type has worked exceptionally well in Japan and Sweden, and it works because everyone is free either to ignore it or to take advantage of the incentives it offers.

Pull planning is not intrusive. It is, to begin with, research oriented. MITI, the Japanese Ministry of International Trade and Industry, conducts research on new and emerging world markets and on the changing Japanese and international economic scene as well. Through its Institute for Developing Economies, Japan studies changing conditions in the third world and looks for growth opportunities for its companies. Because MITI is willing to hire the best minds in Japan and train them, the quality of its work is consistently high and its findings are very well regarded by Japan's private industry.

A Japanese friend of mine, whom I will call Toru, works for MITI and exemplifies that government organization's commitment to excellence. Toru completed his master's degree in economics in Tokyo and then went to work for the Tokyo-based MITI specializing in Japanese exports to developing countries. Because he was bright, MITI sent him to Yale University, and he received a Ph.D. in economics. After returning to Japan, where he put in twelve-hour days six days a week, he began specializing in Japan's relations with Latin America.

Latin America is a priority area for Japan. While we have written off the continent because of its high debt and declining incomes, Japan sees it as an area for future growth. To have better knowledge about Latin America, Toru was frequently sent there to conduct research, meet with government leaders, and sometimes just to walk around and gather facts by talking to the ordinary citizens of the countries of that region.

MITI decided to invest more in Toru and so he was sent to the University of California at Berkeley for postdoctoral studies, then to Columbia University for more study, and finally to Mexico for extensive visits and studies at *El Colegio de Mexico* and the Center for the Study of the Third World. All in all, it took more than three years for Toru to conclude these postdoctoral studies, during which time he received nearly his full salary from MITI. When Toru returned to Tokyo to rejoin his fellow government employees, he did so as someone who could speak with complete authority on the future of Latin America, its relationship with the United States, and its emerging relationship with Japan. As a result of having immersed himself in the cultures of both the United States and Latin America, he also developed a sense for the nuances of each society which he could convey to members of the government or to those pursuing business in the region.

The investment made in Toru by MITI is not unique. Other

researchers from that ministry are pursuing similar studies in Canada, Europe, Africa, the Middle East, throughout Asia, and of course in the United States. Although it is an expensive way to acquire expertise, it has been a very successful way for the Japanese to develop their understanding of new markets and to help their companies compete in those markets.

It goes without saying that we have no governmental research capability equal to MITI's—especially market research. In this era of tax cuts and spending hikes, research grants to members of the Department of Commerce or to the Treasury Department are not high priority. Yet it is precisely this kind of global market research that can help not only business leaders but also Congress to determine priorities and programs for the development of new markets and to begin the assault on the balance-of-trade deficit. We need to develop a well-funded, high-quality think tank on global economic affairs that is every bit the equal of Japan's MITI.

There is another reason our government should sponsor high-quality market research. Small and medium-sized U.S. companies need this research to help boost their exports; most of them are already too lean to support research efforts of their own. At the same time, the majority of the commercial research available, particularly on global markets, is useless, sometimes misleading, and invariably expensive. Companies need to know what markets are emerging and how to reach those markets, and they need enough lead time to prepare their entries into these markets.

Pull planning is not limited to the production of comprehensive research on new markets. Research must also be undertaken to identify the "lead" sectors of the economy—those parts that will contribute most to the growth of the whole—so that we can keep ourselves competitive. For example, during the late 1970s and early 1980s the most important sectors of the economy related to high tech, with silicon chip technology and software development becoming the most important subsectors because of their potential to increase greatly the efficiency of existing technology. Chip and software development together have had a significant impact on the way we use fuel by better controlling the heating and cooling functions in commercial buildings, the way fuel is burned in cars, trucks, trains, and planes, and by giving us the means to allocate electricity consumption more efficiently. This technology has also put powerful design tools in the hands of engineers and architects, and there are countless other applications of this technology as well.

Yet we are beginning to fall behind in chip production and design while other countries have undertaken major software design initiatives. To prevent the outright collapse of some of our major chip-producing companies, the government has intervened to set price limits on imported chips; but it has done so after the fact, without planning. Simply limiting imports does not solve the problem that we have surrendered our lead to the Japanese in one of the most critical areas for the future growth of our country. We should have had enough "early warning" to act before the Japanese began to dominate the market for chips and before our overall balance of trade in high-tech items became negative.

One example will show how fragile our present position in chip manufacturing really is and why we must anticipate problems and opportunities far in advance rather than simply react after the fact. Despite protests by the CIA, the Defense Department, and even IBM, one of our most important technology companies, GCA Corporation, is on the brink of bankruptcy. GCA is vitally important to our future because it is one of only two (the other is Perkin Elmer) remaining U.S. makers of state-of-the-art optical "reducing wafer steppers," those devices that etch miniature circuits on silicon wafers—a basic process in the production of chips. GCA's devices are at the forefront of this technology and their equipment is in use at most of the major chip-producing firms around the country.

But this tiny, independent company must go head-to-head with Japanese optical giants such as Canon, Nikon, and Hitachi, which now dominate the high-tech wafer-stepper market. If GCA goes out of business, as it is feared, then we will be dependent upon only one medium-sized American company to fight it out with Japan's giants. If we lose the last American producer as well, many industry specialists fear the Japanese will not sell us their latest equipment.

Clearly we cannot rely simply on import restrictions in hopes of keeping the economy competitive. We must develop the ability to anticipate new developments and act before our markets are lost. In banking, the FDIC can force a merger between two or more banks that are showing signs of weakness or even temporarily take over a bank to protect the depositors. But when it comes to businesses like GCA, there is no agency with the equivalent of FDIC's power that can shield us from the loss of an industry vital to our country's future.

Good-quality research should be available to track emerging economic and technological developments and to point to areas of vulnerability as well as to areas of opportunity. This research ought to be unbiased, of a consistently high quality, and freely available to help companies in their struggle for market share. If bright, well-trained minds—equal to those at MITI—can point to problems and opportunities we will encounter two or three or even four years from now, we will have come a long way from relying on the "invisible hand."

Traditionally, we have relied on the private sector to undertake such research. Data-base companies, newsletter writers, and specialized information services abound. But simply relying on these providers of information has not enabled us to alter our decline in overall competitiveness, nor has it really helped us in developing and dominating new markets over the long haul. Our collective mentality may be given to flashes of brilliance—as evidenced by the share of Nobel Prizes our nation has won—but it has not been as successful when it comes to such mundane but important matters as protecting the market shares of our automotive, airplane, computer, and even service sector companies. Rather than stand firm ideologically and resist allowing the government to research our future, we should realize that the resources of government, wisely spent, could do much to propel us back into first place.

We also need high-quality research to stimulate investment, research, and training. The Defense Department, the National Institute of Science, NASA, and other federal agencies have all supported vital computer, chip, and software research. In addition, groups of industry leaders have banded together to conduct research on the so-called "fifth-generation" computers and on the possibility of cooperating in producing chips. There are also well-financed research programs in the medical and biological sciences.

But these research programs are all ad hoc and are not part of any larger program or plan of action to enhance America's competitiveness. Each bit of research may advance us a little, but the results would be far more significant if they were coordinated around the twin objectives of bailing out the economy and helping companies become more competitive.

If the president and Congress had an industrial research institution working for them they would have a regular source of very practical domestic and international market information, as well as detailed analyses about which economic sectors have the most significance for the future. And they would receive recommendations for stimulating those lead sectors.

Today Congress and the president receive their information and their policy recommendations from a wide variety of standing and special committees and commissions. Each of these bodies might look at one or two different elements with respect to our global competitiveness and then issue a report on that particular subject. If we are lucky, some of these reports will actually be read, and an important point or two might eventually work its way up from the committee staffs to the politicians themselves. But it is far more likely that the results of these reports will simply fall into oblivion because there is currently no framework in which to put them. I believe, however, that such a framework should be found to make sense of the Congress's and the president's daily research inputs. Furthermore, I believe that the framework we need to concern ourselves with is one that will view the day's findings in terms of global competitiveness and domestic economic strength. Without enhancing either our global competitive position or the strength of our domestic economy, it is unlikely that we will be able to deliver very much of the American Dream to future generations.

A MITI-like, pull-oriented planning organization, preferably at the Cabinet level, is urgently needed. It should be research driven and dedicated to the fundamental concern of keeping America at the forefront of the world's most competitive and important industries. On a periodic basis it should review our domestic economic strengths in an effort to unleash a new era of American industrial growth and development. But to do so it must, at minimum, be able to encourage training, investment, research, manufacturing, and exports. We have come to a point where the weaknesses in our economy are so pronounced that we face the choice of either a rapid acceleration of our current Decline and Crash or an intense mobilization of our resources to become competitive once again.

Achieving an economic renewal in the era of Reaganomics is perhaps impossible. Money must be spent to help business modernize in the growth sectors, and in the current climate no such money is available. Instead, we have embarked on the strange path of spending more on the military, taxing less, and borrowing the difference. These are policies based more on dreams than on realities and they will lead to the impoverishment of future generations. Instead of borrowing heavily to subsidize military consumption, we must balance the books so that we can once again afford to spend money to develop our productive capacity, drive interest rates down, and make the environment a place that favors production over the games of the parasitic corporate raiders. And we must open up new long-term markets for our goods.

A MITI-type, Cabinet-level, Department of Industrial Planning would do well to examine the successes we have had with respect to agriculture. Although our nation has always been blessed with abundant and fertile land, our farmers have not always been the world's most productive. Strange as it may seem, prior to the Russian Revolution in 1917, the breadbasket of the world was not Kansas or Nebraska but the Ukraine.

The successful development of our agriculture was based on the creation of a kind of agricultural MITI within the Department of Agriculture. This novel organization may have applicability to other sectors of the economy as well. Under the Department of Agriculture's benevolent guidance our farmers have increased their yields beyond what was thought possible only a few decades ago. Until the advent of the Reagan administration, when farmers' incomes began to fall, the American farmer was the best-paid agricultural worker in the world. In spite of these high earnings, our farmers were able to sell what they produced on world markets and earn consistently high returns because of their phenomenal and growing rates of worker productivity.

With the assistance of the Department of Agriculture a model system was set up that combined the best of government planning and private enterprise. Beginning in 1862 the government set up a series of agricultural colleges and farm extension offices around the nation that would back research, educate students, and train working farmers in an all-out effort to increase agricultural productivity. Special credit programs were also set up to help farmers finance seed, fertilizer, and equipment purchases even during periods of declining earnings. Other governmental services that were made available included programs to facilitate the export of our farm products and to store grain during times of surplus. And, of course, there were subsidies to persuade farmers that certain crops should be planted over others.

There may have been no set of government programs as successful as those of the Agriculture Department—so much so that its successes must now be reviewed with an eye toward shifting from the production of certain farm commodities, such as grains, which are in surplus, to the cultivation of others, such as vegetables, fruit, and fish, which we do not produce in sufficient quantities. With proper study, there is much to be learned from a century of highly successful incentive farming that can be adapted to the needs of industry. Under the aegis of a U.S. Cabinet-level MITI, the following programs might be undertaken based on the experience of the Department of Agriculture.

American management, especially in the manufacturing sector, is in need of help. Many of our products are not competitive, their quality suffers, and increasingly there are complaints from purchasers about delays in delivery. Many of our largest companies are beginning to address these problems by moving their manufacturing offshore, while our smaller companies are transforming themselves from manufacturers into importers of products made elsewhere.

The time is ripe for the establishment of management and even engineering extension offices similar to the agricultural extension offices that have worked so well. By providing training and assistance—backed up by research—to companies around the country we will soon be able to upgrade our management skills and our productivity. Management extension might not be needed, or sought, by every company, but it would certainly enhance our competitiveness if it were available and staffed by experts with a broad range of technical experience and training. In addition, these centers should help shorten the long lag times between development of a new product, process, technique, or procedure and its widespread use. These centers could also serve as focal points for the systematic collection of valuable information about the state of our manufacturing plants and the level of our management capability. The information gathered could then be used to design new educational and training programs to augment our existing levels of skill and expertise.

Under such a program, we could also make available to U.S. companies the kind of credit and credit-guarantee schemes that we routinely support in the third world through such American-financed organizations as the World Bank. With interest rates currently so high, we are discouraging new investment in this country and encouraging firms to go offshore for their manufacturing. A Federal credit program designed to enhance our competitiveness ought to be sector specific (that is, available only to those industries that will help us become more competitive in the future) and limited to offsetting the difference between today's U.S. interest rates and those available to our top competitors in the same business sectors in Japan and Germany. In this way, the cost of financing an improvement in our competitive position will not be higher than a similar action undertaken overseas. And with the Federal portion of the loan guaranteed, there will be an additional incentive for our banks to make loans for productive pursuits. Such a program, however, must be very closely monitored since banking tends to be among the least responsible sectors of the economy. Financing from such a program also should be limited to the purchase of American-made capital equipment.

To restore competitiveness we must also increase the size of the Federal Export/Import (Exim) Bank. The Exim Bank, which was scaled back during the Reagan administration (in spite of the fact that it makes a profit from financing exports), needs more capitalization, particularly in today's climate, when the sales of big-ticket export products like airplanes are made not just on the basis of technology, price, and delivery, but also on the basis of financing costs. The Exim Bank ought to have enough capital available to lend money to the foreign purchasers of our big-ticket items, such as power-generating equipment, heavy equipment, railroad equipment, and other profitable items. Funding priorities within the Exim Bank ought to be made based on research specifying which sectors are most important for our future. In this way the Exim and other credit programs can pull industry into the future by providing incentives without pushing other firms out of business.

The items just mentioned are the minimum requirements for an American MITI. They will be expensive to provide at first, but as they begin to re-ignite the country's growth they will more than pay for themselves, just as our farm programs have more than paid for themselves by providing years of bountiful crops, high wages for the farmer, big exports, and plenty of inexpensive food for the consumer.

But a Cabinet-level MITI is not enough to end the Decline and Crash. Government must also quickly abandon the suicidal policies of the Reagan years during which we financed our military buildup by borrowing from overseas creditors. If we are to continue to support such a large-scale military presence in the world then we must pay for it through taxation. To do otherwise will only serve to strengthen our military at the expense of the economy.

Because the federal deficit is so large (more than $220 billion added to it in 1986 alone), we have deprived ourselves of some of our most important financial and monetary tools for stimulating the economy during bad times. The longer we remain a debtor nation, the longer will we be threatening to bring down the entire economic system.

We must cut military spending to bring down the size of the budget deficit. One way to do this is by dramatically increasing the efficiency of military procurement, which could save as much as $20 billion to $40 billion out of expenditures of $300 billion for 1988. But the body of the defense budget must also be trimmed, and revenues must be raised, if we are to avoid the complete destruction of our economy.

One of the most painless ways of raising government income is to tax imported oil. With about 2.1 billion barrels of oil imported annually a tax of $8 per barrel would bring in more than $17 billion per year to the Treasury while raising the price of gas at the pump by no more than 7 cents per gallon, according to my estimates.

At the same time, some of the Reagan-era tax cuts must be repealed. According to the Commerce Department, tax revenues of $842 billion are projected for 1987 while budget outlays will total more than $1 trillion, which will increase the federal debt by more than $173 billion. These estimates, which usually project less of a deficit than actually occurs, mean that the federal government will once again have to borrow heavily from abroad to support its spending habits, thus keeping American interest rates high, which serves as a deterrent to investment.

If a 10 percent surcharge ($84 billion) were added to our overall tax bill (with the heaviest proportion of the increase going to the richest 10 percent of the country), this combined with the already mentioned imported-oil tax and savings on the military would reduce the deficit to about $32 billion— still very high, but somewhat more manageable.

It is never easy to raise taxes, especially since it became such an issue during the 1984 presidential campaign when candidate Walter Mondale told the American people he would be forced to increase taxes to bring the economy back to health. Mondale, who probably lost the election with that much too candid remark, predicted that Reagan also would be forced to raise taxes, but he underestimated Reagan's willingness to borrow at the expense of our future economic well-being.

If no politician has the foresight or guts to raise taxes, then we can expect even greater declines in our standard of living and a worsening business climate. If no politician begins to tackle the debt, then our influence in the world will wane as we continue to go on our knees to the Europeans and Japanese for more loans. We will be offering, in return, the protection of their oil as it travels through the Persian Gulf at the expense of American lives.

But how can we get that deficit down and so avoid becoming Europe's and Japan's mercenary? I think we can do this in a very positive way that would also dampen some of the speculative fever in this country that now siphons off so much capital from productive investments. Because an excessive amount of capital is being used to either fight or wage takeover wars, the gains from that type of highly speculative, destructive investment ought to be taxed more heavily. A tax of a 10–15 percent tax on the value of junk bonds issued to buy stocks rather than invest in production might raise another $5 billion to $7 billion while discouraging unproductive takeovers. It would also bring down the deficit to below

$30 billion while greatly strengthening the economy. It is even conceivable that over a period of a few years the defense budget could be shaved by an additional $25 billion or so, which would bring military spending down to the still very sizable 1984 level. In this way the budget could be balanced fairly painlessly and the economy would derive tremendous benefit.

There is one problem, however, with balancing the budget in such a short span of time. With the United States out of the credit markets our interest rates would fall rapidly. As a result, the dollar would decline, and foreigners would be able to gobble up our equity for a fraction of its worth. Or foreign investors might simply flee into other currencies, thus bringing on a bottomless "free fall" in the value of the dollar.

True, exports would also be boosted by a plunge in the value of the dollar if its sole means of support, high interest rates, were eliminated. But who knows just how far such an unsupported dollar might fall if interest rates decline to the 3 percent level that is optimum for growth. If the dollar goes into free fall against the other major trading currencies our buying power would also suddenly decrease. Without the benefit of the huge American market the world's economy would be brought to a grinding halt.

There is a way to prevent a fall in the value of the dollar so that a balanced budget could be achieved with lower interest rates and resumed growth. Back the dollar again with gold, or with another valuable commodity like silver or even platinum, or with a mixed basket of commodities in precisely measured quantities, as proposed by Robert Heller, governor of the Federal Reserve Board.

We are long past the days when we can say that $35 is equal to one ounce of gold. There has been too much mismanagement of our economy and too many dollars printed to set the dollar at that price. But why not say that the dollar can be exchanged at the rate of $450 per ounce of gold, or even $500 per ounce? Then, with the link to gold reestablished, the dollar would again become a store of value and would not fluctuate against the other currencies in such a volatile way.

Of course, many people argue that a dollar/commodity link is too inflexible. They say that such a link would tie the hands of the policy makers in Washington. But that is just the point. It is time to tie the hands of the policy makers who advocate tax cuts on the one hand and spending increases on the other. By removing volatility from the dollar, discipline will be imposed on the rest of the economy.

There is one more element needed to end the Decline and Crash: the creation of new markets as a way to clear the world of its vast oversupply of both commodities and goods. Fortunately, there is such a market waiting to be roused in the form of the debtor developing countries. If our interest rates fall, I believe these countries will have a much better chance of paying off their loans. However, simply lowering the rate of interest is not enough. These countries will still need help if they are to resume their purchases of our products.

One of the most innovative ways of dealing with the third world's debt is to convert it from short- and medium-term bank loans to long-term bonds—a proposal put forward by Brazil's finance minister, Dilson Funaro, as the Crusado Plan, but quickly killed by Treasury Secretary James Baker and Fed chairman Alan Greenspan. With the low prevailing rates of interest and extended terms of bonds, the third world would be able to resume its growth and once more purchase our products—we can even tie the transformation of this debt to the purchase of our products, if we like—while it clears the world of commodity gluts.

If the "securitization" of debt (turning debt into bonds) were to be accomplished, it would also give our banks something valuable, bonds, in lieu of the bad loans they made. On paper the value of the loans and of the bonds would be equivalent so there would be no decline in bank assets as there would be if these countries were to default on their loans. But the big banks would suffer from diminished revenue and a lower return on stockholder equity if this plan were adopted. As a result, their stock prices might fall, but they would be protected from takeovers by the new junk bond tax and—if necessary—new laws as well.

This drop in the value of bank stocks is a small price to pay for getting back the third world, our second largest export market after Canada, and rehiring some tens of thousands of high-wage workers who have lost their jobs as a result of Latin America's decline. Why should we take into account only the profits of the big banks when we consider what to do with the debtor countries of the third world? The issue is more than a banking issue; it involves our exports and the stability of a region as well. After all, the banks made these loans without giving much thought to the long-term value of these countries' commodity assets. Nor did they give enough thought to the level of corruption among the borrowers and to the way in which the money loaned would be used. Our banks were less than prudent in their lending, and this reckless lack of concern for their depositors has brought our own financial system to the edge of instability.

Rather than worry too much about how profitable our banks will be in the future, we ought to seek ways to ensure that third world countries do not default on their outstanding loans. Making these loans secure will go a long way toward stabilizing our economy and will renew our access to a very valuable market as well.

THE foregoing program to end our Decline and Crash will be politically difficult and painful to put into action. There is deep, ideological opposition to planning, even pull planning, just as there is deep opposition to having the government help industry do its job. Compounding this is a deep philosophical divide with respect to cutting the budget, raising taxes, and pegging the dollar to something solid, like gold. Most of all, there is opposition to any plan that will hurt the earnings of our major banks, even if those earnings threaten to exclude us permanently from an important export market.

This set of proposals, though, will work to reverse the Decline and Crash and will do so without destroying the world's trading system. In fact, the plan will do much to restore and stabilize not only our own economy, but the economies of the rest of the world as well.

AS A nation we have been favored with rich lands and industrious people. In a relatively short span of time we have gone from a band of settlers crouched along the Atlantic rim to a nation spanning the continent. Our wealth and power have enabled us to dominate the post–World War II era and our science and technology have allowed us to put our footprints on the moon.

But something is clearly wrong. We emerged from two world wars this century with our cities, towns, and factories unscathed and yet we have been overtaken by the very nations we had vanquished. Japan and Germany, with their smaller populations and meager resources, are pulling far ahead of us in the race to the future.

For too long we have stifled the shouts of those who were warning us that something is not right with our nation. Americans are optimistic people who do not like to be troubled by the stirrings of gloom. Presidents and congressmen have told us not to pay attention to the "nattering nabobs of negativity"—as former vice-president Spiro Agnew called them. But while we refused to acknowledge our problems, they only grew worse.

We are now in dire need of action. We must acknowledge our shortcomings and plan a way to overcome them. In today's Decline and Crash economy, we must produce and export $200 billion more (or consume $200 billion less each year) to balance our trade with other nations. To do this will not be an easy task. The Japanese worker, who is now earning nearly twice what his American counterpart makes, is able to produce higher quality products, ship them half-way around the world, and still sell them for less money than we can. As long as we are unable to match and even better Japan's performance, we will continue to decline.

It is time to awaken from our sleep of Reaganomics. It is time to size up the future with clear minds. It is time to begin planning because the invisible hand has been failing us for at least fifteen years. We have slipped tremendously, but if we act now there is still time to recover our lost ground. There is still time to reassert our leadership, recapture our markets, and create new wealth. If we act without delay, we can resume real growth.

But we must resolve not to delude ourselves. We sit on the edge of a very steep precipice and the ledge beneath us is giving way.

11

PROTECTING YOUR MONEY IN A DECLINE AND CRASH ECONOMY

WHEN the stock market collapsed on October 19, 1987, falling 508 points, it was a symptom of an insidious disease. The disease is the Decline and Crash economy, an economy built on debt with declining wages, offering few real investment opportunities. Money poured into the stock market not simply because we were overtaken by a rise in speculation fever, but also because there were few other places to put money. After all, in a glut economy, people saw no future in investing in overbuilt commercial real estate or in depressed commodities. With factories around the world standing idle and our big Latin American trading partners unable to buy our goods, no one was interested in investing in new machines or technology.

I was advising people to stay away from the stock market as early as March 1987. My advice today is the same. The stock market has become a playground for takeover specialists who exchange corporate assets for debt. It is the butcher's block of the economy where companies are raided, divisions are stripped away, and the nation's productivity is squandered. The rise in stock prices just before the collapse was not a sign of economic strength, but of weakness. And of course, much of the growth in share prices came from the Japanese using their trade surpluses to buy our stocks.

But if you get out of the market, where do you put your money?

After the market's collapse a decision was made by Alan Greenspan and by the central banks of our trading partners to produce "liquidity." Liquidity is money and it is being made available to offset some of the losses from the stock market crash. This means that money is being printed or loaned at low rates to partially make up for the tremendous deflationary shock to the economy brought about by the $1 trillion loss in stock prices. A loss of $1 trillion in the nation's buying power is an enormous amount—equal to about 12 percent of our nation's net worth.

With Greenspan's decision, which is all that he could do given our weakened condition, there is the added risk of inflation. In fact, because interest rates were allowed to fall and the value of the dollar was allowed to collapse, there is no way to avoid renewed inflation.

The resurgence of inflation will hit fairly hard. First, the prices for imported products will jump dramatically. And because we no longer produce many of the products we import (consumer electronics, for example) we will have no choice but to continue buying from overseas sources. This means that the trade deficit will not improve by much, at least in the short term, even as the dollar falls.

With interest rates low, the dollar low, and an infusion of cash rushing into the economy from Greenspan's push for liquidity, the outlook for investments related to real estate is very good, but with two caveats.

Because commercial real estate is overbuilt in all but a few regions, I would avoid it. Only buildings that are large enough to attract the interest of rich foreign investors will be selling. So avoid commercial real estate.

Instead, I recommend investment in apartment buildings

and in single-family homes in the prime areas of the country. Real estate on the West Coast and East Coast would be my first priority, around either the Boston/Washington corridor or the San Diego/Los Angeles/San Francisco axis.

The second caveat is that these properties will not be able to appreciate in value for long. The inflationary jolts that have been delivered to the country will not mean long-term growth. The underlying economy is too weak. This means that housing prices will grow and will hold for two or perhaps three years but, unless the underlying Decline and Crash economy is rectified, potential purchasers of these properties will not have the incomes necessary to sustain their inflated prices. Unless there is a real effort made by the government to end the Decline and Crash, real estate should not be kept later than 1990, when the economy will begin to contract once again after the initial inflationary jolt.

The prudent investor should not go very deeply into debt in order to purchase real estate at this time. Nor would I recommend purchasing a property with a mortgage payment that cannot be sustained by its rental price. In these strange times we must be prepared for both inflation and deflation. For that reason I would suggest putting no more than one-fourth to one-third of your money in real estate, in areas where it is possible to sell property quickly.

The second investment to make during the Decline and Crash is in high-quality government debt. I would put between one-quarter and one-third of my money in ninety-day Treasury notes. Although the interest rates are low at present, eventually they will rise because government debt is not contracting. More important, government debt is still one of the safest places to park your funds.

Do not be too concerned, however, if interest rates fall a little more during the 1988 presidential election. Interest rates usually fall just prior to an election, especially when the chairman of the Federal Reserve Board is appointed by an incumbent. In the current case, Alan Greenspan, a loyal Republican appointed by Reagan, will try to hold down interest rates on federal funds in an effort to stimulate the economy and make the Republicans look good. But the low interest rates that will prevail just before the 1988 election will increase after it, when there is once again the need to support the value of the dollar. After the election, especially if the Republicans win, it is likely that interest rates will rise moderately in an effort to bring inflation levels down. This will increase the attractiveness of Treasury notes as an investment.

I would also recommend putting one-third of your money in a well-managed foreign currency (the Swiss franc is my choice) because the dollar is still overvalued, judging by the trade statistics. This must be done soon to protect your funds, however.

Swiss bank accounts are easy to open—even without going to Switzerland—although some banks require a minimum deposit of $100,000 if the account is opened in the United States. Swiss banks pay low interest rates, between 3 and 4 percent, but the strength of the Swiss currency, which is still linked to gold, makes up for these rates. Like the German mark and the Japanese yen, the Swiss franc gained about 40 percent in value against the dollar during 1987 alone.

And the Swiss franc is one of the best managed, safest currencies around, backed up by the conservative Swiss government, by a rich national economy, and by huge gold and currency assets. The Swiss, unlike the Americans, have been excellent long-term planners and have been able to protect their industries from the competition of Europe as well as Japan while paying the highest wages and providing their workers with the best benefits in the world. As a small, neutral country, Switzerland is also less inclined to change the value of its currency because of political pressure from Washington. The next president may try to squeeze Japan and Germany into keeping the value of their currencies within a certain range against the dollar, but he is not about to pressure the Swiss since we trade so little with that nation.

The remainder of your money should be kept in cash in a safe deposit box, but preferably not in a bank. This money will gain no interest, but if prices fall—which I believe they must after the initial inflation has ceased—then this money will increase in purchasing power. The reason it should not be kept in a bank is because so many of our banks are on the verge of collapse.

I have no doubt that the FDIC, FSLIC, and other government agencies will attempt to bail out these banks. But the question is, when will you get paid? If too many banks go under and the government is hard pressed, you may be paid immediately in long-term bonds, as Texas governor Bill Clements predicted, or you may have to wait years until the government has the cash on hand (the FDIC makes no promises as to when it will pay its depositors).

The strategy I have just outlined is designed to preserve your assets. Even if we elect a new government that decides to take aim at the Decline and Crash and implement a new growth plan for the country, this investment strategy will remain sound. And it will protect your assets until the nation as a whole enters a new period of growth.

But if we continue in the direction of certain decline and large-scale crash, then the above-outlined strategy will serve you even better by protecting your wealth and allowing it to increase.

It is tragic that we must now begin to think seriously about ways to protect our assets and minimize our losses. Throughout the immediate post–World War II years we took growth for granted and prided ourselves on our management of the international system. More than any other country, we were responsible for the postwar system and for its phenomenal vigor—but we are also responsible for its demise.

Now, more than ever, we must create the future. We must renovate the architecture of our nation's economy and plan for its renewal. Anything less will fall far short of what is needed. We must put an end to the Decline and Crash of the American economy, now, before it is too late.

INDEX